DATE DUE			

Days of the Lord

Days of the Lord

I. Winter

Edited by

William G. Storey

HERDER AND HERDER

1965
HERDER AND HERDER NEW YORK
232 Madison Avenue, New York 10016

Original French edition: *Les Jours du Seigneur,* edited by P. Drujon and R. Cappanera, Editions du Témoignage Chrétien, Paris; German edition: *Die Tage des Herrn,* edited by Heinrich Bacht, S.J., Josef Knecht, Frankfurt am Main.

The other volumes of *Days of the Lord* are:
II. Spring
III. Summer and Fall

Grateful acknowledgment is hereby expressed to those publishers who have granted permission to reprint selections from their works. A detailed list of these works appears in the Reference Table at the end of this book.

Nihil obstat: William J. Collins, S.T.L.
Censor Librorum

Imprimatur: ✠ Ernest J. Primeau
Bishop of Manchester
August 4, 1965

Library of Congress Catalog Card Number: 65-21941

Manufactured in the United States of America
By H. Wolff Book Mfg. Co., Inc.

Contents

SANCTORAL

Foreword

Of making books there is no end; so runs the commonplace observation that always sounds like a complaint.

If this be true of other types of books, it is certainly true of books for meditation, including anthologies which profess to bring together the best and holiest moments of the best and holiest minds. Nor is it the mere number of these that frequently warrants complaint; their level of excellence is, in all charity, all too often lamentable.

William G. Storey has brought together out of his wide reading and deep love of the literature of meditation a book which none will lament; its contents leave no ground for complaint. As one of the millions who, lacking creative mystical insights of their own, frequently depend for their meditations on the intuitions of others concerning the wonderful things of God, I find my library shelves and chapel prie-dieu covered with collections of the thoughts of the saints and the reflections of the mystics who seek God, if together they may find Him. Some of these books I have cherished since youth; some became sources of guidance during seminary years; some are limited to treasures of the household of the faith, while others range far afield to bring together testimonies to the primacy of the spiritual and the secret of the good life as these have been perceived by rare souls of every spiritual tradition.

Professor Storey's *Days of the Lord* is easily the best meditation book of its kind to have come to my attention. He has already established himself by other publications among the foremost contributors to the enrichment of the liturgical prayer-lives of contemporary Christians. Now he takes his place among the number of those generous scholars who, recognizing the need for daily meditation in all who constitute the Church, seek to share those riches of the mind, the heart, the very souls of the Church which they themselves bring to the works and the world of their own lay careers.

His publisher speaks of his present work as a "modern breviary for the modern Christian." In further terms associated with the traditional Breviary, it is a kind of *Totum* bringing together good things, true and beautiful, from everywhere within Christendom's space-time dimensions, from the catacombs to today's concentration camps, from the cloister to the hearth, from the Greek and Latin Fathers to the verse of Emily Dickinson, from the sacred Scripture to the constitutions of the Second Vatican Council.

I cannot imagine a happier means to the formation of a truly Christian mind and heart in those who take seriously the priesthood of the laity than the excellent work of Professor Storey that it is my holy privilege to introduce with these few but warmly felt words of appreciation, admiration, and gratitude.

✠ JOHN J. WRIGHT
Bishop of Pittsburgh

Preface

Only the Holy Spirit can teach us to pray as we ought.

The present work has as its sole ambition to cooperate humbly with this activity. It aims at helping the "raising of one's soul toward God" without constraining it in any way.

A line or two from the Mass of the day, usually from a reading of Scripture, is an ample occasion of prayer for many. If, however, meditative prayer does not spring spontaneously from a recollected reading of such lines or from their context in the missal, perhaps a perusal of the texts compiled in *Days of the Lord* will prove of assistance. This is its only aim.

Commentaries are provided for every Sunday, for all the days of Lent, the octaves of Easter and Pentecost, the Ember Days, and for all feasts of the Lord, and for the major feasts of Our Lady, the apostles, and many saints. Those who desire meditative texts for spiritual reading on the ordinary weekdays may turn back to the texts of the preceding Sunday or to those of the nearest feast day.

The Liturgical Year

Holy Mother Church is conscious that she must celebrate the saving work of her divine Spouse by devoutly recalling it on certain days throughout the course of the year. Every week, on the day which she has called the Lord's day, she keeps the memory of the Lord's resurrection, which she also celebrates once in the year, together with his blessed passion, in the most solemn festival of Easter.

Within the cycle of a year, moreover, she unfolds the whole mystery of Christ, from the incarnation and birth until the ascension, the day of Pentecost, and the expectation of blessed hope and of the coming of the Lord.

Recalling thus the mysteries of redemption, the Church opens to the faithful the riches of her Lord's powers and merits, so that these are in some way made present for all time, and the faithful are enabled to lay hold on them and become filled with saving grace.

In celebrating this annual cycle of Christ's mysteries, holy Church honors with especial love the Blessed Mary, Mother of God, who is joined by an inseparable bond to the saving work of her Son. In her the Church holds up and admires the most excellent fruit of the redemption, and joyfully contemplates, as in a faultless image, that which she herself desires and hopes wholly to be.

The Church has also included in the annual cycle days devoted to the memory of the martyrs and the other saints. Raised up to perfection by the manifold grace of God, and already in possession of eternal salvation, they sing God's perfect praise in heaven and offer prayers for us. By celebrating the passage of these saints from earth to heaven, the Church proclaims the paschal mystery achieved in the saints who have suffered and been glorified with Christ; she proposes them to the faithful as examples, drawing all to the Father through Christ, and through their merits she pleads for God's favors.

Finally, in the various seasons of the year and according to her traditional discipline, the Church completes the formation of the faithful by means of pious practices for soul and body, by instruction, prayer, and works of penance and of mercy.

CONSTITUTION ON THE SACRED LITURGY [1]

MAN AND TIME

The day and the year are the primordial units for our measurement of time; in each case, the earth completes a full movement, and such integral cycles can be a symbol of life itself for us, a life which has its morning and its evening, its Spring and its Fall.

Caught up in the natural rhythms of the universe and the world, man can also find in them a rhythm for his soul. Just as the earth receives its energy from the sun, so man finds in the passage of the days and the years dimensions adapted to the successive stages of his spiritual growth.[2]

The daily cycle is one of immediate demands, of indispensable little tasks, of the "terrible duties of everyday." It is the cycle of daily work, of the kind of things that a workman can weigh and count each evening as the tangible fruit of his daily labor, earning him his bread and his bed. The day is the field of ascetical effort, viewed a little naïvely perhaps by one of the Fathers of the Desert in the following way: "Man can attain to divine proportions between sun-up and sundown, if he wants to." [3] With all its limitations and its human preoccupations, the day contains divine possibilities. The daily cycle is also the eucharistic cycle and the cycle of choral prayer, of the hours of the Divine Office, "so that the whole course of the day and night is made holy by the praise of God." [4]

The day may be thought of as a little year, concealing within its twenty-four hours a kind of miniature of the rich varieties of the annual cycle. For men, the year with its four seasons of growth and decline, fecundity and repose constitutes the whole cycle of nature, and is the one great natural unity by which we measure our duration. By means of the year we can situate ourselves in the swift flow of events and capture, as it were, in a framework given us by nature, the shifting kaleidoscope of existence. Like the sower and the reaper, every man must surrender himself in the vast perspective of the turning seasons to something greater and more venerable than himself. Neither the earth nor man can simply turn on its own axis as in the daily cycle; each must turn around a fixed center which measures and disposes in sovereign fashion the phases and the incidents of its progress. The very grandeur of this cycle invites man to the awareness that even the most personal and freest of his actions is inserted in a grand and mysterious and overarching design which is guided from above. Such a complete and mysterious cycle very fittingly stands for the whole of life and of history. Jesus himself, citing Isaiah, referred to His redemptive mission as the proclamation of *the acceptable year of the Lord* [Lk. 4, 19], and more than once cast the history of the world in terms of sowing and reaping, planting and harvesting. [Mk. 4, 3–20, 26–29; Mt. 13, 24–33; Jn. 4, 37–38]

If the secret of human existence lies in a close synthesis of permanency and renewal, we shall find that the annual cycle of the liturgical year fulfills both these requirements. It is a renewal of the abiding mysteries of both the natural and the supernatural worlds; it provides men with a fixed center as well as with those rhythmic revolutions which are his immersion in time.

The old Church knew that life is here our portion, to be lived in fulfillment. The stern rule of Benedict, the wild flights of Francis of Assisi, these were coruscations in the steady heaven of the Church. The rhythm of life itself was preserved by the Church, hour by hour, day by day, season by season, year by year, epoch by epoch, down among the people, and the wild coruscations were accommodated to this permanent rhythm. We feel it, in the south, in the country, when we hear the jangle of the bells at dawn, at noon, at sunset, marking the hours with the sound of Mass or prayers. It is the rhythm of the daily sun. We feel it in the festivals, the processions, Christmas, the Three Kings, Easter, Pentecost, St. John's Day, All Saints', All Souls'. This is the wheeling of the year, the movement of the sun through solstice and equinox, the coming of the seasons, the going of the seasons. And it is the inward rhythm of man and woman, too, the sadness of Lent, the delight of Easter, the wonder of Pentecost, the fires of St. John, the candles on the graves of All Souls', the lit-up tree of Christmas, all representing kindled rhythmic emotions in the souls of men and women. . . . Oh, what a catastrophe for man when he cut himself off from the rhythm of the year, from his union with the sun and the earth. Oh, what a catastrophe, what a maiming of love when it was a personal, merely personal feeling, taken away from the rising and setting of the sun, and cut off from the magic connection of the solstice and the equinox! This is what is the matter with us. We are bleeding at the roots, because we are cut off from the earth and sun and stars, and love is a grinning mockery, because, poor blossom, we plucked it from its stem on the tree of Life, and expected it to keep on blooming in our civilized vase on the table.

D. H. LAWRENCE [5]

Once engaged in the temporal cycles of our history, Christ shall never be a stranger to them again. The Lord of history lives out history in us, but in a victorious way since His death, resurrection, and ascension. *I am with you . . . you in me and I in you . . . forever, unto the end of the ages.* [Mt. 28, 20; Jn. 15, 4–5]

Living for a Christian is sharing in the very life of Christ. It means living again as a penitent, as a reconciled brother, as an heir and member, the very mystery of love toward our heavenly Father and all our brothers. That is why Jesus in making disciples simply associated them with himself and called them to follow Him on His mission. As the Church relives each year her liturgical cycle, she responds again to the invitation addressed to her first members on the banks of the Jordan or of the Lake of Galilee, or in the villages and countrysides of Palestine. The reason for rejoining Jesus each year in this way is not so much in order to have a travelling companion or a model to follow, but rather so that her members can learn how *to put on Jesus Christ* [Rom. 13, 14] by an actual reliving of his saving mysteries.

> Just as the Pagan who contemplated the course of nature, the movement of the stars, the dying of the vegetation in the winter and its rising again in the spring, strove to participate in the divine mystery and to share in the divine life; so the Christian who contemplates the life of Christ, desires to share in that life, to die with him and to rise again to a new and immortal life. This is the mystery which underlies the sacred liturgy. It is a means by which the Christian may share in the life and death and resurrection of Christ.
>
> B. GRIFFITHS [6]

[1] *Constitution on the Sacred Liturgy,* December 4, 1963, Chapter V, numbers 102, 103, 104, 105; Glen Rock, New Jersey, Paulist Press, 1964.

[2] As early as the third century, St. Cyprian of Carthage established a parallel between the stages of the spiritual life and the succession of the seasons (*Letter* 37, 2).

[3] Quoted by M. Viller, *La spiritualité des premiers siècles chrétiens,* p. 66.

[4] *Constitution on the Sacred Liturgy,* Chapter IV, number 84.

[5] D. H. Lawrence, cited in *The Catholic Worker,* June, 1963, p. 7.

[6] B. Griffiths, *The Golden String,* New York, P. J. Kenedy, 1954, p. 140.

Temporal

O God,
each year you gladden us
with the expectation of our redemption;
grant that,
as we joyously welcome your only-begotten Son
coming as our Savior,
we may receive him without dread
when he comes as our Judge.
(*Collect, Christmas Eve*)

WINTER SOLSTICE

These are the days when birds come back,
A very few, a bird or two,
To take a backward look.
These are the days when skies resume
The old, old sophistries of June,
A blue and gold mistake.
O fraud that cannot cheat the bee
Almost thy plausibility
Induces my belief.
Till ranks of seeds
Their witness bear,
And softly through the altered air
Hurries a timid leaf.
O Sacrament of summer days,
O Last Communion in the Haze,
Permit a child to join.
Thy sacred emblems to partake,
Thy consecrated bread to take,
And thine immortal wine.

EMILY DICKINSON [1]

Advent

Advent is both a beginning and an end, an alpha and omega of the Church's year of grace. Too often considered merely a season of preparation for the annual commemoration of Christ's birth, this rich and many-layered season is actually designed to prepare the Christian for the glorious possibilities of the Parousia.[1] It is a season of longing expectation—*Come, Lord Jesus!* [Ap. 22, 20]—during which Isaiah,[2] the "evangelist" of the Old Testament, and John the Baptist,[3] the immediate herald of the Lord, proclaim in insistent terms the Messiah's coming in history and mystery. The revelation of Jesus the Christ in the Christmas-Epiphany mysteries—however wonderfully and tenderly portrayed in Christian tradition and sentiment—is considered but a prelude to the coming of Christ in glory and in judgment, an event which dominates all the readings of Advent.

From this point of view, Advent is, although "decidedly ambivalent in character," [4] more the completion of the mysteries of Christ and the *end* of the liturgical year than its beginning. Al-

[1] "*Adventus*" is the exact Christian Latin equivalent of the Greek "*parousia.*" By Advent we mean the whole season that climaxes in the feast of the Epiphany or Theophany. Cf. H. A. Reinhold, *The Dynamics of the Liturgy,* New York, Macmillan, 1961, p. 63.

[2] The Roman Liturgy uses selections from the Book of Isaiah at Matins each day of Advent and in the Masses of the Advent Ember Days.

[3] The Gospels of the last three Sundays of Advent feature the Baptist very prominently.

[4] *Worship,* 38, November-December, 1964, p. 673.

though the Church's year has come to have two poles or foci, it must be understood that, in fact, there is only one cycle of mysteries, revolving about Easter. The manifestation of Christ which we await while meditating on how he first appeared among us will be the final revelation of his transforming and transfiguring resurrection. *Behold, I make all things new . . . Behold, I come quickly*. [Ap. 21, 5; 22, 12]

COME, LORD JESUS!

FIRST SUNDAY OF ADVENT

Now is the time to rise from sleep. (Epistle)

Advent is the time for rousing. Man is shaken to the very depths, so that he may wake up to the truth of himself. The primary condition for a fruitful and rewarding Advent is renunciation, surrender. Man must let go of all his mistaken dreams, his conceited poses and arrogant gestures, all the pretenses with which he hopes to deceive himself and others. If he fails to do this, stark reality may take hold of him and rouse him forcibly in a way that will entail both anxiety and suffering.

The kind of awakening that literally shocks man's whole being is part and parcel of the Advent idea. A deep emotional experience such as this is necessary to kindle the inner light which confirms the blessing and the promise of the Lord. A shattering awakening; that is the necessary preliminary. Life only begins when the whole framework is shaken. There can be no proper preparation without this. It is precisely in the shock of rousing while he is still deep in the helpless, semi-conscious state, in the pitiable weakness of that borderland between sleep and waking, that man finds the golden thread which binds earth to heaven and gives the benighted soul some inkling of the fullness it is capable of realizing and is called upon to realize.

ALFRED DELP [2]

The twofold coming.

What we proclaim is not one single coming of Christ, but a second as well, much fairer than the first. For the first presented a demonstration of long-suffering, but the second wears the crown of the Kingdom of God. Most things about our Lord Jesus Christ are twofold. His birth is twofold, once of God before the ages, and once of the Virgin in the end of the ages. Twice he comes down, once all unseen like dew on a fleece, and a second time still future and manifest. When first he came, he was swaddled in a manger. When next he comes he will *clothe himself with light as with a garment.* [Ps. 104, 2] At his first coming *he endured the cross despising the shame* [Heb. 12, 2]; at his second, he comes surrounded with glory and escorted by hosts of angels. We do not therefore simply rest upon Christ's first coming, by itself, but let us look forward also to his second; and as we say of his former coming, *Blessed is he that comes in the name of the Lord* [Mt. 21, 9], so also we will say the same words again at his second coming, that we may meet our Master in company with angels and say, "Blessed is he that comes in the name of the Lord" as we worship him. The Savior comes again, but not to be judged again, for he will pass judgment on those who passed judgment on him, and he who aforetime kept silence as they judged him now reminds those lawless men who did their outrageous deeds to him upon the cross, and says, *These things hast thou done, and I kept silence.* [Ps. 50, 21] He adapted himself when he came then, and taught men by persuasion, but this time it is they who will be forced to bow to his rule, whether they will or no.

ST. CYRIL OF JERUSALEM [3]

During this period of expectation, who is waiting for whom—man for God or God for man?

To love anybody is to expect something from him, something which can neither be defined nor foreseen; it is at the same time in some way to make it possible for him to fulfill this expectation. Yes, paradoxical as it may seem, to expect is in some way to give:

but the opposite is none the less true; no longer to expect is to strike with sterility the being from whom no more is expected; it is then in some way to deprive him or take from him in advance what is surely a certain possibility of inventing or creating. Everything looks as though we can only speak of hope where the interaction exists between him who gives and him who receives, where there is that exchange which is the mark of all spiritual life.

GABRIEL MARCEL [4]

The Kingdom of God is at hand. (Gospel)

We live always during Advent, we are always waiting for the Messias to come. He has come, but is not yet fully manifest. He is not fully manifest in each of our souls; He is not fully manifest in mankind as a whole: that is to say, that just as Christ was born according to the flesh in Bethlehem of Juda so must He be born according to the spirit in each of our souls.

The whole mystery of the spiritual life is that Jesus is forever being born in us. We have got to be always transforming ourselves into Christ, taking on the dispositions of His heart, the judgments of His mind; for the whole meaning of being a Christian is to become bit by bit transformed into Jesus Christ, so that we truly become children of His Father, for the only real children of the Father are those who have fully "put on" the Son, and the mystery of the Christian life is that each soul becomes Christ.

In the same way Christ has not fully come in regard to mankind as a whole; though He has come in certain peoples, He has not come in others. There are whole stretches of humanity in which Christ has never been born. The mystical Christ is not yet complete. He is still incomplete, lacking members, and the perfect missionary prayer is for Christ to come in the whole world, for His body to attain its fullness of stature.

JEAN DANIELOU [5]

For some, God is He who lets us sleep, He who speaks the words of assurance which dispense them from all searching. For others, God is He who snatches from us that "false peace" in which, according to Pascal, the world dwelt before Christ's coming.

HENRI DE LUBAC [6]

There are two kinds of people one can call reasonable; those who serve God with all their heart because they know Him, and those who seek Him with all their heart because they do not know Him.

BLAISE PASCAL [7]

SECOND SUNDAY OF ADVENT

May the God of hope fill you with all joy and peace in believing, so that you may always be filled with hope by the power of the Holy Spirit. (Epistle)

Now hope, says God, now there's something that astounds me.
Me, even me.
It is truly astonishing,
How these children of mine see the way things are going and yet believe that somehow tomorrow things will be better.
How they see the way things are going today and believe they'll be better tomorrow morning.
It's really astonishing and the greatest marvel of our grace.
I'm astonished at it myself.
It means that my grace must be of unbelievable power.
And that it must flow from an inexhaustible source like a great river.
Since the first time it began to flow and for all the time it has been flowing—
In my natural and supernatural creation
In my spiritual and corporeal creation
In my eternal and temporal creation
Mortal and immortal creation—
Since that first time—O that first time!—when it flowed like a river of blood from the pierced side of my Son.

What grace, what power in my grace in order that little hope, flickering before the breath of sin, trembling in every wind, disturbed by the least draught,
Should also be so unwavering, faithful, straight, and pure; so unconquerable, immortal, and impossible to extinguish:
This little sanctuary light, which burns forever in its faithful lamp.
A candle flickering amidst the darkness of the worlds.
A candle glowing across the length of the ages.
A candle shining fitfully through the depths of the nights.
Since that first time when my grace flowed for the creation of the world.
For all the time that my grace has been flowing for the conservation of the world.
Since that time that the blood of my Son flowed for the salvation of the world.
A flame which is impossible to extinguish, even death cannot blow it out.
Hope is what astonishes me, says God.
I can't get over it.
Little hope, whom one would hardly notice,
My little daughter hope,
She is immortal.

CHARLES PEGUY [8]

Christian hope has God for its object, and it need not surprise us that God is also its origin. Some people think that Christian hope is an extension of natural hope, that it is simply natural hope equipped by the believer's faith with a wider range which enables it to go beyond the frontiers of this world and embrace the beyond. In their eyes, this grant of the plenitude of happiness after death—this respite for the unsatisfied, the disappointed, the despairing—is the fruit of personal optimism, so irrepressible that only eternity can come up to the measure of its dreams. It is just a matter of temperament—you can look either at this life or at the next through rose-tinted glasses. In other words, they say, the hope of the sons of God is simply the passional hope of the children of man, distinguished from the latter by its objects, which are strictly supernatural, and is the special reserve of those who were born with an invincible optimism.

A. M. CARRE [9]

The Forerunner lived in the kind of expectation which prepares the way of the Lord in each man's soul: John in his prison had heard of Christ's deeds and sent two of his disciples to say to him: "Are you the one who is to come?" (Gospel)

Can we now picture to ourselves this first appearance of the Baptist? He came into a world with an ancient tradition, with a belief, a conviction, that a great future lay before it, yet where both tradition and belief were marred by the dross that had gathered round them. He came among men intent upon their own affairs, especially their own political affairs, in consequence suspicious, self-centred, prone to hatred. Religion for them was a rigid, stereotyped substitute form; against its claims and ever-growing tyranny many had long since begun to chafe, though they could not lay aside the old inheritance, nor rid themselves of its ceremonial, nor reject altogether the hope in the future which it gave. He came at a time when many, eager souls as well as souls that feared, were on the tip-toe of expectation, strained so far that they were in danger of despair. He came and stood in the desert by the river, at the gateway leading into Judaea, on the very spot that was still hallowed by the memory of the prophet Elias, hard upon the main road along which the busy world had to pass; a weird, uncouth, unkempt, terrible figure, in harmony with his surroundings, of single mind, unflinching, fearing none, a respecter of no person, asking for nothing, to whom the world with its judgements was of no account whatever though he showed that he knew it through and through, all its castes and all its colours. He came the censor of men, the terror of men, the warning to men, yet winning men by his utter sincerity; telling them plainly the truth about themselves and forcing them to own that he was right; drawing them by no soft inducements, but by the hard lash of his words, and by the solemn threat of doom that awaited them who would not hear; distinguishing true heart-conversion from the false conversion of conformity, religion that lived in the soul from that sham thing of mere inheritance and law; going down into the depths of human nature in his ceaseless search for *the true Israelite in whom there was no guile* [Jn. 1, 47]; an angel and no man, a fearless voice to which the material world seemed as nothing; compelling attention, fascinating even those who would have passed him by, making straight the path through the hearts of men; cleansing, baptizing, pointing to truth of life, but as yet, until all was prepared, saying nothing of that Lord whose coming he was sent to herald, content to foretell only the Kingdom; John, the focus upon which all the gathered light of the Old Dispensation converged, from which was to radiate the light of the New.

ALBAN GOODIER [10]

Go tell John what you have heard and seen. (Gospel)

Jesus did not separate the gospel from miraculous cures. They are similar deeds; by that answer he meant that he had cured bodies in order that the souls might be better disposed to receive the gospel.

Those who did not see the light of the sun can now see the light of truth; those who did not hear even the words of men can now hear the words of God; those who were possessed of Satan are freed from Satan; those who were foul and ulcerated are clean as children; those who could not move, who were strengthless and shrunken, now follow my footsteps; those who were dead to the life of the soul have risen at a word from me . . . and the poor, after the Good News, are richer than the wealthy. These are my credentials, my letters proving my legitimacy.

GIOVANNI PAPINI [11]

THIRD SUNDAY OF ADVENT

THE HOLINESS OF THE CHURCH

Your voice speaks:

In my arms I still carry flowers from the wilderness, the dew on my hair is from the valleys of the dawn of mankind.

I have prayers that the meadows lend an ear to, I know how storms are tempered, how water is blest.
I carry in my womb the secrets of the desert, on my head the noble web of ancient thought.
For I am mother to all Earth's children: why do you scorn me, world, when my Heavenly Father makes me so great?
Behold, in me long-vanished generations still kneel, and out of my soul many pagans shine toward the infinite.
I lay hidden in the temples of their gods, I was darkly present in the sayings of their wise men.
I was on the towers with their star-gazers, I was with the solitary women on whom the spirit descended.
I was the desire of all times, I was the light of all times, I am the fullness of all times.
I am their great union, I am their eternal oneness.
I am the way of all their ways, on me the millennia are drawn to God.

GERTRUDE VON LE FORT [12]

But you, for your part, will be no longer in the shadow but in the glory of the Light inaccessible; you will be in the City that is yours because you helped to build it; you will see Him at last as He is, and be wholly with Him; and you will have no more any mourning or weeping or any other sorrow, for all these former things will have been transmuted into happiness and peace, and you will walk with Him—together with all those you have helped to bring to Him, even until the end of the world—you will walk with Him in happiness for ever, in the cool of the eternal evening.

GERALD VANN [13]

He confessed: I am not the Messiah. (Gospel)

John the Baptist had the great joy of knowing that his testimony was heard, as those who had been his disciples recognized Christ. He had prepared the way, and now John, Peter, James, the disciples he had prepared, recognized Christ when He came. John showed Him to them as the Lamb of God. And there lay John's great joy—the joy of seeing the bride meeting the Bridegroom. That was all he wanted. His one wish was to lead souls to Christ, take them to meet Him. At that moment of meeting his joy was complete. When his disciples left him to follow Christ it was perfect. He wanted nothing else. It was he who had come to prepare the way of the Lord. He had no wish to keep any souls for himself. In this he is the perfect model of self-denial. He never wanted anyone to grow attached to him—his one wish was to attach everyone to Christ. Having once prepared the way, he then faded out himself to leave them with the Bridegroom, with Christ.

And there you have the chief thing we must keep in mind concerning him: he was the man whose love expressed itself in disinterested zeal—that is to say, we see it less from his delight in Christ's personal presence, for after all from this he was often separated, than from his perfect fidelity in carrying out the missions he had been given, and thus leading souls to Christ. It is this that gives his love its special character. It consisted chiefly in wanting Christ to feel the joy of having souls, of finding more and more souls brought to Him. It was for this that Christ thirsted. It was this that John worked for. He took more delight in giving Christ joy than in himself enjoying Christ—if I may put it so. This means that there must have been some most special grace of love given him. He was indeed the servant whose love was, above all, expressed by serving, doing whatever Christ wanted, whatever Christ commanded. Serving perfectly. Our Lord wants His servants to be like that. *I have found a man after my own heart, who does all that I ask of him* as we read in a verse of a psalm. [See Acts 13, 22] There are so few men Christ can make free with. The souls He loves most are those He can make free with, those of whom He can ask whatever He wants, souls which are His to dispose of. Now John the Baptist was, above all, a man who put himself completely into our Lord's hands, the perfect servant who did what his master wanted, whose joy was to hear the Bridegroom's voice.

JEAN DANIELOU [14]

EMBER WEDNESDAY IN ADVENT

The Winter Ember Days, older than Advent itself, contain a strong emphasis on the first coming of Christ in the nativity mysteries, whereas the Sundays of Advent proclaim the messianic and final coming of the Savior. The Golden Mass (Missa aurea) *of Ember Wednesday celebrates with special joy the initial coming of Emmanuel: God-with-us.*

Mary and Eve.

Just as it was through a virgin who disobeyed that man was stricken and fell and died, so too it was through the Virgin, who obeyed the word of God, that man resuscitated by life received life. For the Lord came to seek back the lost sheep, and it was man who was lost; and therefore He did not become some other formation, but He likewise, of her that was descended from Adam, preserved the likeness of formation; for Adam had necessarily to be restored in Christ, that mortality be absorbed in immortality, and Eve in Mary, that a virgin, become the advocate of a virgin, should undo and destroy virginal disobedience by virginal obedience.

ST. IRENAEUS [15]

An angel chieftain was sent from Heaven to greet the Forthbringer of God with Hail! Then seeing thee, O Lord, take flesh he is wonder-rapt, and standing crieth out with no lips of flesh to her:

Hail! by whom true hap has dawned.
Hail! by whom mishap has waned.
Hail! sinful Adam's recalling.
Hail! Eve's tears redeeming.
Hail! height untrodden by thought of men.
Hail! depth unscanned by angels' ken.
Hail! for the kingly throne thou art.

Hail! for who beareth all thou bearest?
Hail! O star that bore the Sun.
Hail! the womb of God enfleshed.
Hail! through whom things made are all new made.
Hail! through whom becomes a Babe their Maker.
Hail! through whom the Maker is adored.

HAIL! BRIDE UNBRIDED.

THE AKATHISTOS HYMN [16]

EMBER FRIDAY IN ADVENT

The Visitation.

Mary, bearing the sacred Presence, like the Ark of the Covenant, journeys to Judaea to pay a visit to the house of Zachariah which was to last three months. The Son of God who is within her and the Holy Spirit which overshadows her, like the glory and the cloud which indwelt and overshadowed the sanctuary, drive her with haste to her kinswoman Elizabeth. The Virgin is consumed with the desire to communicate to her relatives, who are also the poor of Yahweh, the Good News of the messianic greeting. The text of the prophet Isaiah floods into her mind in the presence of this vision:

> *How beautiful upon the mountains are the feet of him who brings good tidings, who publishes peace, who brings good tidings of good, who publishes salvation, who says to Zion, your God reigns.* [Is. 52, 7]

St. Paul applies this text to the preacher of the Gospel [Rom. 10, 15], but may we not see in Mary the first bearer of the Gospel of the Incarnation and Redemption? With speed, she bears the good news to the hill country, as it were to Zion, to Zechariah and to Elizabeth—the news that God reigns according to the very word of the angel: *The Lord God will give to Jesus the throne of David his father; he shall reign over the house of Jacob for ever and his rule shall never end.* [Lk. 1, 32f.] Mary carries to Judaea the news of peace, good will, and salvation. This haste and this joy of Mary well illustrate the mission of the Apostles and the Church after her. Indwelt by the Holy Spirit, bearing the Word and the Body of Christ, the Church has only one desire and one joy and that is to transmit them to all men that they may share peace, good will, and salvation by a proclamation of God's rule.

The entry of Mary into the house of Zechariah and the greeting which she directs to Elizabeth appear as a revelation of God himself, like some miraculous epiphany. Mary's greeting echoed in the ears of Elizabeth like a voice coming from God and gives rise in her to a sense of miraculous wonder. John the Baptist, in her womb, leaps with joy, according to the messianic prophecy: *But for you who fear my name the Sun of righteousness shall rise with healing in his wings. You shall go forth leaping like calves from the stall.* [Mal. 4, 2] John the Baptist is like David who danced and leapt with joy before the Ark of the Covenant at the entering-in of Jerusalem. [2 Sam. 6, 16; 1 Chr. 15, 29] The Son of God in Mary produces in her a kind of messianic exaltation, even as the sacred Presence in the Ark calls King David to dance and tumble with joy. *And Elizabeth was filled with the Holy Spirit.* [Lk. 1, 41] The word of Mary is heard as the Word of God; John the Baptist, the Forerunner, in spite of his unborn state, trembled with joy; Elizabeth had been filled with the Holy Spirit. The word of Mary, on account of the Messiah whom she bears, is made one with the very Word of God, producing the miracle of the awakening of the Forerunner by messianic rejoicing and the gift to his mother of the spirit in abundance. Mary here appears for the first time as one intimately linked with the mission of the Son of God; she is indeed the Mother of the Lord. Mother and Son are made one; the word of the mother conveys the Word of the Son, she transmits the Spirit of God, and produces a divine miracle in Elizabeth. This unity of Mother and Son emphasizes very strongly the reality of the Incarnation: God has truly taken flesh in the Virgin Mary, is the Son of Mary, and Mary is the Mother of God.

MAX THURIAN [17]

Mary and Eve.

In accordance with this design, Mary the Virgin is found obedient, saying, *Behold the handmaid of the Lord, be it done unto me according to thy word.* [Lk. 1, 38] But Eve was disobedient; for she did not obey when as yet she was a virgin. And even as she, having indeed a husband, Adam, but being nevertheless as yet a virgin, having become disobedient, was made the cause of death both to herself and the whole human race; so also did Mary, having a man betrothed (to her) and being nevertheless a virgin, by yielding obedience, became the cause of salvation, both to herself and the whole human race. And on this account does the law term a woman betrothed to a man the wife of him who had betrothed her, although she was as yet a virgin; thus indicating the back reference from Mary to Eve, because what is joined together could not otherwise be put asunder than by inversion of the process by which these bonds of union had arisen, so that the former knots be cancelled by the latter, that the latter set the former again at liberty. And it has in fact happened, that the first compact looses from the second tie, but that the second tie takes the position of the first, which had been cancelled. For this reason did the Lord declare that the first should in truth be the last, and the last first. And the prophet too indicates the same, saying, *Instead of fathers, children have been born unto thee.* [Ps. 44, 17] For the Lord, having been born *the First-begotten of the dead* [Col. 1, 18] and receiving into his bosom the ancient Fathers, has regenerated them unto the life of God, he having been made himself the beginning of those that live, as Adam became the beginning of those who die. Wherefore also Luke, commencing the genealogy with the Lord, carried it back to Adam, indicating that it was he who regenerated them into the gospel of life, and not they him. And thus also it was that the knot of Eve's disobedience was loosed by the obedience of Mary. For what the virgin Eve had bound fast through unbelief, this did the virgin Mary set free through faith.

ST. IRENAEUS [18]

EMBER SATURDAY IN ADVENT

I shall send my messenger before you to prepare your way. (Gospel)

Since Christ is forever "He who is to come," since the whole history of the Church, from Ascension day to the Last Judgment, is the history of His Parousia in the hidden world of men's souls, John is also forever going before Him, because the pattern of things in Christ's Incarnation is the pattern for everything that happens in His Mystical Body. Just as every grace comes to us through Mary, because she could not have borne Christ without being equally the mother of His Mystical Body, so in every conversion the way has been prepared by John the Baptist. That was the teaching of the Fathers. "I think," wrote Origen, "that the mystery [*sacramentum*] of John is still being carried out in the world. If a man is to believe in Jesus Christ, the spirit and power of John must first come into his soul and prepare for the Lord a perfect people, make the rough ways of the heart plain, make the crooked straight. Even now the spirit and power of John precede the coming of our Lord and Savior."

Since the coming of Christ goes on forever—He is always He who is to come in the world and in the Church—there is always an Advent going on, and this Advent is filled by John the Baptist. It is John the Baptist's peculiar grace that he prepares the way for what is about to happen. It belongs to him specially to be there for the final preparation before every spiritual unfolding, every missionary development, every missionary awakening; and this grace of his is at work now. He it is who hastens the coming of Christ by sending out his resounding call to repentance, to conversion; and the power of his call makes men ready for Christ to come to them. It seems to me that we ought to feel this call of his as most specially pressing today, when for some countries at least this coming of Christ seems so urgent and so near.

JEAN DANIELOU [19]

FOURTH SUNDAY OF ADVENT

Stir up our hearts, O Lord, to prepare the coming of your only-begotten Son. (Collect)

Here is the moment to conquer the melancholy of time, here is the moment to say softly and sincerely what we know by faith. This is the season for the word of faith to be spoken in faith: "I believe in the eternity of God who has entered into our time, my time. Beneath the wearisome coming and going of time, life that no longer knows death is already secretly growing. It is already there, it is already in me, precisely because I believe. For the cycle of birth and death to stand still in the true reality all I have to do is believe in the coming of God into our time, really believe. In the act of believing, I patiently bear with time, with its hard and bitter demand that brings death in its wake. And I dwell no longer on the thought that time has the last word to say, which is a denial.

"Listen, my heart, God has already begun to celebrate in the world and in you his Advent. He has taken the world and its time to his heart, softly and gently, so softly that we can miss it. He has even planted his own incomprehensible life in this time (we call it his eternity and we mean thereby that which is nameless, which is wholly other from the time that makes us so hopelessly sad). And this is precisely what happens in you yourself, my heart. It is called the grace of faith, the grace of the gradual falling away of fear of time, of the fear that fades away because he who is more powerful than time (which he made to be redeemed into eternity) has done great things to it. A now of eternity is in you, a now that no longer has any denial before it or behind it. And this now has already begun to gather together your earthly moments into itself.

"No brighter joy could be expected by you, poor heart, in a season of Advent that lasts for a lifetime (since *your* advent will end only when you hear the words, 'enter into the joy of your Lord'). No brighter joy, for now you still feel too keenly the harsh press of the shackles of time, even though they have already begun to fall away from your hands and feet. The only thing that must live in you is a humble, calm joy of faithful expectancy which does not imagine that the tangibles of the present time are everything. Only humble joy, like the joy of the prisoner, who will stand up even while he is still imprisoned, because, lo and behold, the bolt has already been torn off the door of his dungeon, and so freedom is already guaranteed.

"Is this joy, this Advent joy so difficult? Is resignation and hidden despair really easier? Childish, stubborn defiance and willed malice: that is what despair and resignation amount to. You rightly recognize these, my heart, only when you run away from them, only when you do not dawdle and dispute with them. Only the heart that really does not want to enjoy them, but instinctively recoils and runs from them under the impulse of that eternal life that we call grace—only such a heart can recognize them. But perhaps you don't quite know whether you have chosen Advent joy or the despair of winter that leads to cold death? Just to ask such a question is a mistake, because we can never be neutral about this when we ask it. And to give the second answer would be death, the death that man cannot free himself from.

"Ask not, doubt not. You have, my heart, already chosen the joy of Advent. As a force against your own uncertainty, bravely tell yourself, 'It is the Advent of the great God.' Say this with faith and love, and then both the past of your life, which has become holy, and your life's eternal, boundless future will draw together in the now of this world. For then into the heart comes the One who is himself Advent, the Boundless Future who is already in the process of coming, the Lord himself, who has already come into the time of the flesh to redeem it."

KARL RAHNER [20]

He shall bring to light what is hidden in darkness. (Epistle)

The Majesty of the Son of God, Who is equal to the Father, when clothing itself with the lowliness of a servant, neither feared diminution nor needed increase; and by the sole power of Godhead could effect that operation of its own mercy, which it was bestowing on the restoration of man, so as to rescue from the yoke of a dreadful tyrant the creature formed after God's image. But since the devil had not so proceeded by sheer force against the first man, as to draw him over to his own side without consent of his free will, therefore in such sort were that voluntary sin and that hostile design to be destroyed, as that the gift of grace should not clash with the rule of justice. Accordingly, amid the universal ruin of the whole human race, there was but one remedy which, under the mysterious law of the Divine procedure, could come to the aid of the prostrate; and that was, if some son of Adam could be born, unconnected with original transgression, and innocent, who could benefit the rest both by his example and by his merit. But as natural generation did not allow of this, and the offshoot of a vitiated root could not be without that seed of which Scripture says, *Who can make him clean who was conceived of impure seed? is it not Thou Who art alone?* [Job 14, 4] The Lord of David became the Son of David, and from the fruit of the promised sprout arose an unvitiated offspring, by the combination of two natures into one Person; so that by the same conception and the same childbearing was born our Lord Jesus Christ, in Whom were present both very Godhead for the performance of miracles, and very Manhood for the endurance of sufferings.

ST. LEO THE GREAT [21]

Prepare the way of the Lord. (Gospel)

It was John's mission—and greatness—to proclaim the advent of the kingdom. Nor was he in any way unworthy to do so, he who *even from his mother's womb* [Lk. 1, 15] was filled with the Holy Spirit. It could only mean that his particular vocation was to lead the way to the promised realm, to direct others to it, but in some special sense to remain without. One is reminded of Moses close to death, standing on Mount Nebo and looking down on the Promised Land. He is not allowed to enter. Not until he has passed through death does he come into the true land of promise. For Moses this was punishment; he had failed in an hour of trial. For John it was not punishment but vocation. Everything in him cried out to be with Christ, in that kingdom of

God about to dawn in Messianic abundance, ushering in the new creation. For us its bliss is unimaginable, but for the prophet, who had felt it deeply, it was the object of his most powerful longing. Yet he was not allowed to enter. No psychology, indeed no one who has not personally penetrated deep into the mystery of the divine will, can explain this. This side of death, John was to remain Precursor: herald of the kingdom.

ROMANO GUARDINI [22]

God so loved the world
that he gave his only Son
that whoever believes in him should not perish
but have everlasting life.
[John 3, 16]

Christmas

Christmas is the mystery of giving. God's great gift is no longer promised and awaited, but given and received with joy and gladness. Because of the personal presence of God among us (Emmanuel), mankind is renewed and rejuvenated [1] by an *aggiornamento* which is that of the fresh and eternal youthfulness of Christ himself.[2]

God's gift—a participation in his own life—can be received only by faith. In his Letter to the Romans which is read at Matins of Christmastide, St. Paul dwells on this grand theme in unmistakable words and incomparable force. Mary was the first to welcome the Messiah and His messianic gifts by faith. [*Blessed is she who has believed,* Lk. 2, 45.] Joseph unhesitatingly embraced God's puzzling ways in pure faith. Little by little, others came forward—a handful of shepherds enveloped in heavenly light, a few Magi following a star, some old folk in the temple moved by the interior flame of the Holy Spirit—to acknowledge the *light which shines upon us this day* (Introit, Dawn Mass), *the brightness of God's glory* (Epistle, Day Mass), *the true light that enlightens all mankind* (Gospel, Day Mass), *the light which enlightens the nations and the glory of your people Israel* (Gospel, February 2). Lessons, antiphons, responses, all shine with hidden splendor, letting the eyes of the heart discern the divine mystery concealed and revealed under the most humble appearances, within the tranquil intimacy of an obscure family.

Henceforth, we know God by sight.[3] Christmas teaches men the simplicity of the Infinite; divine life is a newborn Babe lying in a manger with the purity, love, and joy of His guardians as His only companions. The Word became flesh and was thus rendered speechless in His babyhood. Divine life takes on human dimensions, descends to our level, makes itself accessible to those who will, in and with Jesus their Brother, become the children of their heavenly Father. Long before St. Theresa of the Child Jesus, the modern apostle of spiritual childhood, St. Leo the Great preached a series of eloquent Christmas sermons celebrating the sublimity of the Incarnation.[4]

Because the Word became flesh, all flesh is, in a sense, divinized, and the simplest realities of our daily lives take on divine proportions. The Son of God comes to us and adopts us as his brothers and sisters in the midst of our everyday activities. Family life, its emotions, and the deepest sentiments of the human heart are all consecrated in their depths. The liturgy depicts the Incarnation as a marrying of God and man,[5] as a marriage fruitful in sons and daughters of a common Father.

This family life in Christ is destined to embrace and include all. The solemn manifestation mysteries of Epiphany are a final expression of the magnificent prophecies of the Old Testament. Bethlehem and Nazareth are the dawn of a new day which will assemble at high noon all nations in a Jerusalem which will be a true messianic "City of Peace." There will be consummated that "wondrous exchange"[6] of human and divine things when the redeemed respond to the divine generosity by the joyful consecration of themselves and the world to the Father in the Son and through the Holy Spirit.

Neither Christmas nor Epiphany shine, however, with full radiance. Blazing light hardly befits a cradle! Both are still presages

[1] The prayer presently used at the Offertory, "O God, who in a wonderful way created and ennobled human nature, and still more wonderfully renewed it . . . ," is an ancient Christmas collect adapted to other uses.

[2] Epistle of the Mass of Christmas Day (Heb. 1, 1-11).

[3] *"Dum visibiliter Deum cognoscimus."* Preface of Christmas.

[4] For centuries selections from these homilies have been used at Matins of Christmas and of its Octave (January 1).

[5] See the Antiphon for the Canticle of Zachary, January 6.

[6] See the First Antiphon of Vespers and Lauds of January 1 and February 2.

of future and greater things to come. Meanwhile, the mysteries of the infancy are not completely untouched by sorrow. Joyful mysteries they are indeed, and the liturgy breathes a spirit of rejoicing echoing the triumphant song of the angels. And yet, Simeon let Mary and Joseph glimpse what was to come; Jesus was not just to be a Light and a Glory but, alas!, also a sign of contradiction, a stumbling block, and an offense.[7] A blood-thirsty Herod driven by fear and egotism, the massacre of the Holy Innocents, the wailings of Rachel, a precipitous flight by night, and exile for the holy family in a land of idolatry and unbelief are integral parts of the Christmas story. Even Christmas cannot be unadulterated joy for a Savior *who came unto his own, and his own received him not.* [Jn. 1, 11]

O wondrous exchange!
The Creator of the human race,
having assumed a living body,
deigned to be born of a Virgin,
and becoming man without man's aid,
enriched us with his divinity.
(*Antiphon, Vespers, January 1*)

DECEMBER 24
THE VIGIL OF CHRISTMAS

THE PROCLAMATION OF THE NATIVITY

In the year 5199 from the creation of the world, when in the beginning God created the heaven and the earth;
In the year 2959 from the flood;
In the year 2051 from the birth of Abraham;
In the year 1510 from the going forth of the people of Israel out of Egypt under Moses;
In the year 1032 from the anointing of David as king;
In the 65th week, according to the prophecy of Daniel;

[7] Gospel, Sunday within the Octave of Christmas.

In the 194th Olympiad;
In the year 752 from the foundation of the city of Rome;
In the 42nd year of the reign of the Emperor Octavian Augustus;
In the sixth age of the world, while the whole earth was at peace
—JESUS CHRIST, eternal God and Son of the eternal Father;
Willing to consecrate the world by His gracious coming;
Having been conceived of the Holy Ghost, and the nine months of His conception being now accomplished;
Was born in Bethlehem of Juda of the Virgin Mary;
Made Man.
The birthday according to the flesh of our Lord
JESUS CHRIST.

ROMAN MARTYROLOGY [23]

HYMN

Hail Mary,
full of grace;
the Lord is with you,
the Holy Spirit too.
Your priests shall be robed in justice,
they that honour you shall rejoice and exult.
For David's sake, your servant, Lord,
save, Lord, your people, bless your chosen portion.

Hail to the glorious virgin,
Mary, full of grace.
The Lord is with you.
Blessed you are above all other women
and blessed is the fruit of your womb:
for he you conceived was Christ, the Son of God,
and he has redeemed our souls.

COPTIC LITURGY [24]

DECEMBER 25
THE BIRTH OF THE LORD

In giving us his Son, God gave us everything. By delivering up to us his unique Word, he revealed everything to us. There is nothing further to wait for after Jesus Christ.

ST. JOHN OF THE CROSS [25]

To all who received him he gave the power of becoming children of God. (Gospel, Mass of the Day)

Although that infancy, to which the majesty of the Son of God refused not to stoop, advanced with increasing years to full-grown manhood; and, since the triumph of the Passion and Resurrection was completed, all the acts of that lowliness, which was put on for our sakes, have passed away; yet does this day's festival renew for us the sacred beginnings of the life of Jesus, born of the Virgin Mary; and while we adore our Saviour's birth, we are found to be celebrating our own origin. For the generation of Christ is the starting point of the Christian people, and the birthday of the Head is the birthday of the Body. Although each of those whom He has called has his own sphere, and all the children of the Church are distinguished by succession of times, yet the whole number of the faithful, sprung from the font of Baptism, as they are crucified with Christ in His Passion, and raised to life in His Resurrection, and placed at the Father's right hand in His Ascension, so are born with Him in His Nativity. For every one of the believers in any part of the world who is regenerated in Christ has the line of that old nature in which he was born, cut short, and passes by a second birth into a new man; nor is he now reckoned as belonging to the stock of his natural father, but as an offshoot of the Saviour, Who became the Son of Man for this end, that we might be able to be sons of God. For unless He had come down to us by His condescension, no man by any merits of his own could have attained to Him. On this point, therefore, let not earthly wisdom bring any darkness over the hearts of those who are called; nor let the dust of earthly thoughts, which is soon to return to the depths, lift up itself against the loftiness of the grace of God. That which was arranged before the endless ages was accomplished in the world's closing period; prefigurative signs came to an end, and in the presence of realities law and prophecy became truth: that Abraham might become a father of all nations, and in his seed might be given to the world the promised blessing; and the character of Israelites might not belong only to those whom flesh and blood had begotten, but the whole body of the adopted ones might come into possession of the inheritance prepared for the children of faith. Let no idle questionings produce clamorous misrepresentation; nor let human reason criticise the carrying out of a Divine work. With Abraham we believe God, *and stagger not through unbelief,* but *know with full assurance that what the Lord has promised, He is able also to perform.* [Rom. 4, 20-21]

ST. LEO THE GREAT [26]

Blessed is he who comes in the name of the Lord. . . . The Lord has done this and it is marvelous in our eyes. (Gradual, Dawn Mass)

The Second Person "came" into his own: into the world which he had created. Let us consider carefully what this means: the everlasting, infinite Creator not only reigns over or in the world but, at a specific "moment," crossed an unimaginable borderline and personally entered into history—he, the inaccessibly remote one! . . .

According to the Bible, God entered into time in a specific manner, acting on an autocratic decision made in complete freedom. The free, eternal God has no destiny which is a matter for mortals living in history. What is meant is that God entered into history, thus taking destiny upon himself.

However, this journey of God from the everlasting into the transitory, this stride across the border into history, is something no human intellect can altogether grasp. The mind might even oppose the apparently fortuitous, human aspect of this interpretation with its own "purer" idea of godliness; yet precisely here lies hidden the kernel of Christianity. Before such an unheard of thought the intellect bogs down. Once at this point a friend gave me a clue that helped my understanding more than any measure of bare reason. He said: "But love does such things!" Again and again these words have come to the rescue when the mind has stopped short at some intellectual impasse. Not that they explain anything to the intelligence; they arouse the heart, enabling it to feel its way into the secrecy of God. The mystery is not understood, but it does move nearer, and the danger of "scandal" disappears.

None of the great things in human life springs from the intellect; every one of them issues from the heart and its love. If even human love has its own reasoning, comprehensible only to the heart that is open to it, how much truer must this be of God's love! When it is the depth and power of God that stirs, is there anything of which love is incapable? The glory of it is so overwhelming that to all who do not accept love as an absolute point of departure, its manifestations must seem the most senseless folly.

ROMANO GUARDINI [27]

THE NATIVITY OF CHRIST

This is the month, and this the happy morn,
Wherein the Son of Heaven's eternal King,
Of wedded Maid and Virgin Mother born,
Our great redemption from above did bring;
For so the holy sages once did sing,
    That he our deadly forfeit should release,
And with his Father work us a perpetual peace.

That glorious form, that light unsufferable,
And that far-beaming blaze of majesty,
Wherewith he wont at Heaven's high council-table
To sit the midst of Trinal Unity,
He laid aside; and here with us to be,
    Forsook the courts of everlasting day,
And chose with us a darksome house of mortal clay.

JOHN MILTON [28]

Christ our Brother will judge His brothers.

Let us then, according to the light given us, praise and bless Him in the Church below, whom Angels in heaven see and adore. Let us bless Him for His surpassing loving-kindness in taking upon Him our infirmities to redeem us, when He dwelt in the inner-most love of the Everlasting Father, in the glory which He had with Him before the world was. He came in lowliness and want; born amid the tumults of a mixed and busy multitude, cast aside into the outhouse of a crowded inn, laid to His first rest among the brute cattle. He grew up, as if the native of a despised city, and was bred to a humble craft. He bore to live in a world that slighted Him, for He lived in it, in order in due time to die for it. He came as the appointed Priest, to offer sacrifice for those who took no part in the act of worship; He came to offer up for sinners that precious blood which was meritorious by virtue of His Divine Anointing. He died, to rise again the third day, the Sun of Righteousness, fully displaying that splendour which had hitherto been concealed by the morning clouds. He rose again, to ascend to the right hand of God, there to plead His sacred wounds in token of our forgiveness, to rule and guide His ransomed people, and from His pierced side to pour forth His choicest blessings upon them. He ascended, thence to descend again in due season to judge the world which He has redeemed—Great is our Lord, and great is His power, Jesus the Son of God and Son of man. Ten thousand times more dazzling bright than the highest Archangel, is our Lord and Christ. By birth the Only-begotten and Express Image of God; and in taking our flesh, not sullied thereby, but raising human nature with Him, as He rose from the lowly manger to the right hand of power, —raising human nature, for Man has redeemed us, Man is set above all creatures, as one with the Creator, Man shall judge man at the last day. So honoured is this earth, that no stranger shall judge us, but He who is our fellow, who will sustain our interests, and has full sympathy in all our imperfections. He who loved us, even to die for us, is graciously appointed to assign the final measurement and price upon His own work. He who best knows by infirmity to take the part of the infirm, He who would fain reap the full fruit of His passion, He will separate the wheat from the chaff, so that not a grain shall fall to the ground. He who has given us to share His own spiritual nature, He from whom we have drawn the life's blood of our souls, He our brother will decide about His brethren. In that His second coming, may He in His grace and loving pity remember us, who is our only hope, our only salvation!

JOHN HENRY NEWMAN [29]

SUNDAY WITHIN THE OCTAVE OF CHRISTMAS

It was *when all things were in quiet silence,* we are told, that the *almighty Word leapt down* from God's *royal throne* [Wis. 18, 14–15] and became man; it was in the quiet silence of his own soul, while all external things were in tumult and clamour, that the Word came to the consummation of his earthly journey; and this inwardness is of immediate significance for ourselves: the Christian journey is essentially an inner struggle and transformation, and we shall never be transfigured, never become apparelled in celestial light, if we try to escape the struggle by projecting or externalizing it, pretending that the darkness lies only outside us, in the *selva oscura,* the dark wood, of an external and alien world, not inside us, in our own blindness, our own pride and lusts and greeds.

GERALD VANN [30]

This is the drawing-up of our faith, the foundation of the building, and the consolidation of a way of life. God, the Father, uncreated, beyond grasp, invisible, one God the maker of all; this is the first and foremost article of our faith. But the second article is the Word of God, the Son of God, Christ Jesus our Lord, who was shown forth by the prophets according to the design of their prophecy and according to the manner in which the Father disposed; and through Him were made all things whatsoever. He also, *in the end of times* [Dan. 11, 13], for the recapitulation of all things, is become a man among men, visible and tangible, in order to abolish death and bring to light life, and bring about the communion of God and man. And the third article is the Holy Spirit, through whom the prophets prophesied and the patriarchs were taught about God and the just were led in the path of justice, and who *in the end of times* has been poured forth in a new manner upon humanity over all the earth renewing man to God.

ST. IRENAEUS [31]

Sons and heirs of God through Christ.

This design of God's mercy and justice, though overshadowed in previous ages by certain veils, was yet not so much hidden as to be closed to the understanding of holy men, who lived praiseworthy lives from the beginning even to our Lord's Advent. For the salvation which was to come in Christ was promised both by the words of prophets and the significance of events, and was obtained not only by those who preached it, but by all those who believed the preachers. For it is one faith which justifies the Saints of all times; and to the self-same hope of the faithful pertains all that either we acknowledge to have been done, or our fathers hailed as to be done, by the Mediator between God and men, Jesus Christ. Nor is there any distinction between Jews and Gentiles; for, as the Apostle says, *circumcision is nothing, and uncircumcision is nothing, but the keeping of the commandments of God* [1 Cor. 7, 19], which, if we keep them with integrity of faith, make us true sons of Abraham, that is, complete Christians, as the same Apostle says: *For whosoever of you have been baptized into Christ, have put on Christ. There is no Jew nor Greek, there is no bondman nor free, there is no male nor female, for you are all one in Christ. And if you are Christ's then are you Abraham's seed, and heirs according to the promise.* [Gal 3, 27–29].

ST. LEO THE GREAT [32]

A sword of division.

Lord Jesus Christ, I adore you, God eternal, Lord of life and history and of our hearts. You are my life's choice, you and nothing else. I confess that you, Jesus of Nazareth, poor, humble and human, are the Eternal Word, the sword which compels all mankind to a choice. . . .

I confess that you are the Word through whom everything was made, that is made. You are the creator of atomic power, you are the Lord of the human body and of its secrets. To you is judgement given, you are the arbiter over all human justice. You are the Logos, mysteriously at work in all ages in the minds of men. Wherever something of truth was apprehended or something of beauty formed, you were present. All beauty, be it of earth or of heaven, is contained in you alone. And the day will come when you will appear, the splendour of your Godhead irradiating your humanity, to tell all the human race: *I am Alpha, I am Omega, the beginning of all things and their end, says the Lord God; he who is, and ever was, and is still to come, the Almighty*. [Ap. 1, 8]

But the darkness is still with us. You are still hidden and the world which you have made does not want to know you or receive you. There is still war between you and the adversary. For you have come to undo the work of the devil. You have come to bring not peace but a sword. Down the centuries of history and into the very fastnesses of my own heart rings the truth of the words spoken of you, when you were taken as an infant to the temple: *Behold this child is destined to bring about the fall of many and the rise of many and to be a sign which men will refuse to acknowledge*. [Lk. 2, 34] You are still the hidden child in a world grown old. You took human flesh humbly, inviting faith, not compelling it. You are still obscured by the veils of this world's history, you are still destined not to be acknowledged in the scandal of your death on the cross, you are still hidden in the bosom of your visible Church and dumb in the oppressive stillness of your Sacrament. The world knows you not, it overlooks you, and when it does acknowledge you, it despises you or idly spurns you.

But I, O hidden Lord of all things, boldly affirm my faith in you. In confessing you, I take my stand with you, the rejected King of this world, despised in human history, utterly unknown by your own creation. Yet I take my stand, too, with you, who alone among men could say: *Take courage I have overcome the world*. [Jn. 16, 33] If I make this avowal of faith, it must pierce the depths of my heart like a sword; I must bend my knee before you, saying: I must alter my life. I have still to become a Christian. You, O Christ, must give to my earthly existence the final secret meaning, which will constantly reshape my life.

HUGO RAHNER [33]

OUR LADY'S LULLABY

Upon my lap my Sovereign sits,
And sucks upon my breast;
Meanwhile, His love sustains my life,
And gives my body rest.
Sing lullaby, my little Boy.
Sing lullaby, my life's Joy.

When thou hast taken thy repast,
Repose, my Babe, on me;
So may thy Mother and thy Nurse
Thy cradle also be.
Sing lullaby.

My Babe, my Bliss, my Child, my Choice,
My Fruit, my Flower, and Bud,
My Jesus, and my only Joy,
The Sum of all my good.
Sing lullaby.

The fruit of death from Paradise
Made thee exilèd mourn;
My fruit of life to Paradise
Makes joyful thy return.
Sing lullaby.

The shepherds left their keeping sheep
For joy to see my Lamb;
How may I more rejoice to see
Myself to be the Dam.
Sing lullaby.

Three kings their treasure hither brought
Of incense, myrrh and gold,
The heaven's Treasure and the King
That here they might behold.
Sing lullaby.

One sort an angel did direct;
A star did guide the other;
And all the fairest Son to see
That ever had a mother.
Sing lullaby, my little Boy.
Sing lullaby, my life's Joy.

RICHARD VERSTEGAN [34]

DECEMBER 26

ST. STEPHEN THE MARTYR

Peter got his name from a rock because by the firmness of his faith he was the first to deserve to be a foundation of the Church. Similarly, Stephen got his name from a crown because he was the first to deserve to undergo the conflict for the name of Christ, the first to merit to inaugurate martyrdom by that bloodshed so characteristic of the soldiers of Christ. Let Peter retain his long-standing headship of the Apostolic College. Let him unlock the kingdom of heaven for those who enter it, bind the guilty by his power, and mercifully absolve the repentant. But Stephen is the first of the martyrs. Let him be the leader of that purpled army, for he was an eager warrior who shed his blood for the still warm blood of his Lord.

He procured for himself a purple robe, dyed with his own blood. Therefore, later on, he rightly received a crown from his King. And this was he who at his birth got his name from a crown. Clearly, God foreknew and predestined him; now He called him as the first one to come to the glory of martyrdom.

ST. PETER CHRYSOLOGUS [35]

Consider also one thing of which you have probably never thought. Not only do we at the feast of Christmas celebrate at once Our Lord's Birth and His Death: but on the next day we celebrate the martyrdom of His first martyr, the blessed Stephen. Is it an accident, do you think, that the day of the first martyr follows immediately the day of the Birth of Christ? By no means. Just as we rejoice and mourn at once, in the Birth and in the Passion of Our Lord; so also, in a smaller figure, we both rejoice and mourn in the death of martyrs. We mourn, for the sins of the world that has martyred them; we rejoice, that another soul is numbered among the Saints in Heaven, for the glory of God and for the salvation of men.

Beloved, we do not think of a martyr simply as a good Christian who has been killed because he is a Christian: for that would be solely to mourn. We do not think of him simply as a good Christian who has been elevated to the company of the Saints: for that would be simply to rejoice: and neither our mourning nor our rejoicing is as the world's is. A Christian martyrdom is no accident. Saints are not made by accident. Still less is a Christian martrydom the effect of a man's will to become a Saint, as a man by willing and contriving may become a ruler of men. Ambition fortifies the will of man to become ruler over other men: it operates with deception, cajolery, and violence, it is the action of impurity upon impurity. Not so in Heaven. A martyr, a saint, is always made by the design of God, for His love of men, to warn them and to lead them, to bring them back to His ways. A martyrdom is never the design of man; for the true martyr is he who has become the instrument of God, who has lost his will in the will of God, not lost it but found it, for he has found freedom in submission to God. The martyr no longer desires anything for himself, not even the glory of martyrdom. So thus as on earth the Church mourns and rejoices at once, in a fashion that the world cannot understand; so in Heaven the Saints are most high, having made themselves most low, seeing themselves not as we see them, but in the light of the Godhead from which they draw their being.

T. S. ELIOT [36]

To be one with Christ *in via* means to journey through darkness in other senses besides that of the obscurity of faith. The

Door opens on to life, but to life through death. *Fons quasi sepultura est,* says St. Ambrose: the baptismal waters are the "fountains springing up into the life which is eternal," but "the font is tomb" as well as womb; by baptism, St. Paul tells us, we are buried with Christ in his death so as to be raised up like him and with him into a new mode of existence. For some, as for the blessed Stephen, it is literally through the acceptance of physical death for and with and in Christ—a giving up of one's life, whether in martyrdom or in some other mode of self-sacrifice, which is the final act of faith and love—that the heavens open and the Glory is seen; for most, it is the transfiguring effect of the various metaphorical forms of death or darkness they encounter on their way that brings the journey to its conclusion. But for all those who have truly given their faith to Christ, if the way lies through darkness because of its pains and sorrows, it is also a journeying in light, and there is joy in believing, because they look forward, humbly and in fear yet eagerly and with the confidence of hope, to the fulfilment of the promise, the dawning of the eternal day; and also because, even here and now, they know that they walk in the presence and companionship of the Light even though its glory is never fully visible and often seems to be completely hidden from their eyes.

GERALD VANN [37]

DECEMBER 27
ST. JOHN THE EVANGELIST

In his old age at Ephesus Blessed John the Evangelist could barely be supported into Church on the arms of his disciples nor could he say more than a few words when he got there. At each service he would only repeat: "My little children, love one another." Finally the disciples and brothers who were present, wearied by such constant repetition, said to him: "Master, why do you always say the same thing?" The reply was worthy of John: "Because it is the Lord's command, and if you do only this, it suffices."

ST. JEROME [38]

We know he is celebrated for his declarations about Christian love. *Beloved, let us love one another, for love is of God. If we love one another, God dwelleth in us, and His love is perfected in us. God is love, and he that dwelleth in love dwelleth in God, and God in him.* [1 Jn. 4, 7, 12, 16] Now did he begin with some vast effort at loving on a large scale? Nay, he had the unspeakable privilege of being the friend of Christ. Thus he was taught to love others; first his affection was concentrated, then it was expanded. Next he had the solemn and comfortable charge of tending our Lord's Mother, the Blessed Virgin, after his departure. Do we not here discern the secret sources of his especial love of the brethren? Could he, who first was favoured with his Saviour's affection, then trusted with a son's office towards His Mother, could he be other than a memorial and pattern (as far as man can be), of love, deep, contemplative, fervent, unruffled, unbounded?

JOHN HENRY NEWMAN [39]

John now comes forward, a man crying out from heaven and sending forth a voice more sonorous than thunder. He has reached the whole world, has taken possession of it and has filled it with his cry, not by loudly lifting up his voice, but by uttering his words with the aid of divine grace.

It is truly a wondrous thing that the sound, though so great, is not harsh or discordant, but sweeter and more pleasing than all musical harmony, and also more capable of soothing. Besides all this, it is very holy, and most awful, and teeming with such great mysteries, and productive of so many benefits, that those who receive them with eagerness and preserve them with care are no longer merely men. They do not even remain upon the earth, but rise superior to everything belonging to this life and change their state to that of the angels, so that they dwell on earth as if in heaven.

It is the Son of Thunder, the Beloved disciple of Christ, the pillar of all the churches in the world, who now comes to us. It is he who possesses the keys of heaven, who has drunk the chalice of Christ, and has been baptized with His baptism, and who so confidently reclined on the breast of the Lord. He is not taking part in a play, or concealing his head by a mask (for he will not discourse on topics suited to this). He is not mounting the platform, or beating time on the stage floor with his foot, nor is he decked out in golden raiment, but he enters clad in a garment of indescribable beauty. He appears to us, having *put on Christ* [Rom. 13, 14], his beautiful *feet shod with the readiness of the gospel of peace* [Eph. 6, 15], wearing a girdle, not about his breast, but around his loins; a girdle, not fashioned of purple leather or coated with gold, but woven and composed of truth.

It is not as one playing a part that this man now appears to us, for there is no pretense in him, or make-believe, or legend, but with head uncovered he preaches the naked truth. . . .

He has all heaven for his stage; for theatre, the world; for audience, all the angels, and also as many men as are already "angels" or even desire to become so. For only these would have the ability to hear this harmony correctly, and to show it forth in their works, and to be the kind of listeners which the occasion demands. All the rest, like little children, listen without understanding what they hear, but are distracted by cakes and childish playthings. So also they who laugh, fare sumptuously, and live for wealth and power and sensuality, hear what is said, but give evidence of nothing great or noble in their works, because they have become completely preoccupied with brick-making and clay.

The powers above stand by this Apostle, astounded at the beauty of his soul, and his understanding, and the bloom of his virtue, in consequence of which he attracted even Christ Himself and received the grace of the Spirit. Having prepared his soul as a golden-toned lyre, well-made and inlaid with precious stones, he brought it about that the Holy Spirit should send forth a great and sublime sound by its means.

Accordingly, let us listen no longer as to the fisherman, the son of Zebedee, but as to the One who *knows the deep things of God* [1 Cor. 2, 10], I mean the Holy Spirit, as He strokes this lyre. In truth, he will speak nothing human to us, but will draw whatever he may say, from deep spiritual reserves, from those awesome mysteries which even the angels did not know, before they took place. They also have learned by the voice of John, along with us, and through us they have acquired knowledge of what we have learned.

ST. JOHN CHRYSOSTOM [40]

DECEMBER 28
THE HOLY INNOCENTS

Firstfruits of God and the Lamb. (Epistle)

The children of Bethlehem share the scene with our Lord. And the mystery of the words "all this happened—*because the Lord came,*" applies particularly to them. They were not martyred because of the power of a frightened and insane tyrant—that is made quite clear. And we see how completely all life is in the possession of our Lord. It is not mere pious sentiment to call the Child *kyrios.* Our concept of God must retain its grandeur and become firmer. Then the love we profess will also be strong, effective, reliable.

The mystery of the innocents is that they are the victims. The divine eagle gathered them as booty to himself. The blow aimed by the tyrant at our Lord fell on them instead. They serve as a kind of guard of honour to the divine Child—and the militant dialogue between God and anti-God in which they are caught up earns them heaven. But we have lost our awareness of that ceaseless duel; we so little realise that we have a share in the struggle that we ignore it completely. Yet no one can escape responsibility and at any moment God, exercising his sovereign power, may draw us into the thick of it. So far as an adult is concerned this can only lead to salvation if the victim voluntarily accepts the combat and enters it on God's side. But in the case of the innocents the manger sealed their fate and was sacrifice enough. That is their mystery.

And it is also their message and judgment. We have become insensitive to the sovereignty of God. Even where awareness of it still exists a clear cut concept of the relationship and of the order to which it belongs is lacking. The God under whose inexorable law we exist has been dissolved in a mist of psychological outpourings, subjective living conditions or collective existential needs. This is one of the worst evils of our time.

ALFRED DELP [41]

THE FLIGHT INTO EGYPT

Alas! our Day is forced to fly by night!
  Light without light, and sun by silent shade.
O nature, blush! that sufferest such a wight,
  That in thy sun this dark eclipse hath made;
Day to his eyes, light to his steps deny,
That hates the light which graceth every eye.

Sun being fled the stars do less their light,
  And shining beams in bloody streams they drench;
A cruel storm of Herod's mortal spite
  Their lives and lights with bloody showers doth quench:
The tyrant to be sure of murdering one,
For fear of sparing Him doth pardon none.

O blessed babes! first flowers of Christian spring,
  Who though untimely cropp'd fair garlands frame,
With open throats and silent mouths you sing
  His praise whom age permits you not to name;
Your tunes are tears, your instruments are swords,
Your ditty death, and blood in lieu of words!

ROBERT SOUTHWELL [42]

They cram themselves full of experience, they say; they gain experience; they learn about life; from day to day they accumulate experience. A singular treasure, God says.
Treasure of emptiness and want.
Treasure of the seven years' famine, treasure of emptiness and withering and of growing old.
Treasure of wrinkles and anxieties.
Treasure of the lean years. Increase that treasure, God says. In empty granaries
You heap up the empty sacks

Of an empty Egypt.
You increase the treasure of your troubles and your miseries.
And the sacks of your cares and your pettiness.
You acquire experience, you say, you increase your experience.
You are always going downwards, God says, you are always growing less, you are always losing.
You are always going downhill. You are always growing withered and wrinkled and older.
And you will never climb up the hill again.
As for what you call experience, your experience, I call it waste, diminution, decrease, the loss of hope.

And I call it a pretentious wasting,
The diminution, the decrease, the loss of innocence.

And a perpetual degradation.

For it is innocence which is full and experience which is empty.
It is innocence which wins and experience which loses.

It is innocence which is young and experience which is old.
It is innocence which grows and experience which shrinks.

It is innocence which is born and experience which dies.
It is innocence which knows and experience which does not know.

It is the child who is full and the man who is empty.
Empty like an empty pumpkin and like an empty barrel.

There, God says, that is what I think of your experience.

CHARLES PEGUY [43]

DECEMBER 29

ST. THOMAS OF CANTERBURY

Because of his opposition to his former friend, King Henry II of England, who was encroaching on the liberties of the English

Church and its primate, Thomas Becket, Archbishop of Canterbury, was assassinated in his cathedral on December 29, 1170. From the time he had been promoted to the primacy of England by the favor of Henry II, Thomas had offered his life for the sake of the Church.

I am ready to die for my Lord, that in my blood the Church may obtain liberty and peace.

ST. THOMAS OF CANTERBURY [44]

Batter my heart, three person'd God; for, you
As yet but knocke, breathe, shine, and seeke to mend;
That I may rise, and stand, o'erthrow mee, and bend
Your force, to breake, blowe, burn and make me new.
I, like an usurpt towne, to'another due,
Labour to'admit you, but Oh, to no end,
Reason your viceroy in mee, mee should defend,
But is captiv'd, and proves weake or untrue.
Yet dearly I love you, and would be loved faine,
But am betroth'd unto your enemie:
Divorce mee, 'untie or breake that knot againe;
Take mee to you, imprison mee, for I
Except you' enthrall mee, never shall be free,
Nor ever chast, except you ravish mee.

JOHN DONNE [45]

Given the tempo of the liturgical season, with its feasts of the Octave Day of the Birth of the Lord, the Epiphany, the Holy Family, and the Holy Name, it is easy to overlook that one saint who for many centuries was, after Mary and Joseph, the most venerated person in European Christendom. I mean St. Thomas of Canterbury, whose now suppressed feast occurs on December 29.

He was martyred in the year 1170 and canonized two years later, according to the custom of that time.

Devotion to him spread like wildfire. He was enshrined in the hearts of men, and in their arts. In statues and stained glass, in song and story this good bishop was everywhere to be found: France, Italy, Spain, Sweden. Many miracles were attributed to his heavenly advocacy.

History has two names for him, Thomas à Becket and Thomas of Canterbury, but he liked to call himself Thomas of London. The pilgrims in Chaucer's *Canterbury Tales* were of course on their way to the tomb of St. Thomas—a place of pilgrimage almost as celebrated as Rome or the holy sepulchre itself. In 1538, Henry VIII decanonized him saying he was "not a saint, but a rebel and a traitor to his prince."

St. Thomas's mother taught him "sweetly to invoke the Blessed Virgin as the guide of all his ways and the patron of his life," putting all his confidence in her, after Christ.

As a boy she would weigh him in a balance-scale against food, clothes, and alms to be given to the poor.

School in London, back at twenty-two to become a merchant's clerk, with hunting and hawking as his diversions; off to study law again in Italy and France. He was a dazzlingly successful young man of the world, untouched it seems by its grosser vices (despite the portrait of him given us by the inventive screenwriter Edward Anhalt in Jean Anouilh's *Becket*).

At twenty-four he became counselor to Theobald of Canterbury, deacon at thirty-six; just then Henry became king and made him Lord High Chancellor of England. In this office he treated rich and poor alike. He continued to display the aristocratic virtue of magnificence, and he took the lead in battle in France. Yet one day he was found praying in front of a church before dawn. For eight years he was the King's good friend. When the possibility of his being offered the archbishopric of Canterbury was first rumored he said: "Our great love would turn to black hatred." St. Thomas was distinguished, when he came to hold that high office, by his love for the poor; by his tears at the Mass; by the hair shirt he wore under his churchman's ermine.

Thomas à Becket has a lot of company halfway along the road. We would be friends of Christ, yet enjoy life to the full. Someday—someday we know we will have to make a choice. Early in life or late, the decision must come. Christ is a jealous lover. He brooks no rivals.

No one can make us as happy as He, and no one exacts so high a price.

GERARD S. SLOYAN [46]

JANUARY 1
OCTAVE DAY OF CHRISTMAS

Today's feast commemorates the ritual circumcision of the Divine Child, a son of Abraham, and the sacred covenant established between Yahweh and all the children of Israel. It was also on this day that He received the name Jesus, previously given to Him by an angel at His conception. In addition, this is the oldest feast in the Roman liturgy commemorating and emphasizing the role of the Blessed Virgin Mary in God's plan of salvation.

He is born of the Virgin, in order that the disobedience caused by the serpent might be destroyed in the same manner in which it had originated. For Eve, an undefiled virgin, conceived the word of the serpent, and brought forth disobedience and death. But the Virgin Mary, filled with faith and joy, when the angel Gabriel announced to her the good tidings that the Spirit of the Lord would come upon her, and the power of the Highest would overshadow her, and therefore the Holy One born of her would be the Son of God, answered: *Be it done unto me according to Thy word.* [Lk. 1, 38] And, indeed, she gave birth to Him, concerning whom we have shown so many passages of Scripture were written, and by whom God destroys both the serpent and those angels and men who have become like the serpent, but frees from death those who repent of their sins and believe in Christ.

ST. JUSTIN MARTYR [47]

Jesus, God and man.

Since in our Lord Jesus Christ, the true Son of God and man, we acknowledge a Divine nature from His Father, and a human substance from His Mother; although there is but one Person of God the Word and of the flesh, and both essences have acts in common, yet must we take notice of the character of the works themselves, and discern, by the gaze of a pure faith, to what heights the lowliness of infirmity is promoted, and to what depths the loftiness of power stoops down: what it is which the flesh does not without the Word, and what it is which the Word effects not without the flesh. For without the power of the Word, the Virgin would neither conceive nor bear; and without the reality of the flesh, the Infant would not lie wrapt in swathing bands. Without the power of the Word, the Magi would not adore a Child made known to them by a new star; and without the reality of the flesh, there would be no command to remove into Egypt the Child Whom Herod was desiring to kill. Without the power of the Word, the Father's voice sent forth from heaven would not say, *This is My Beloved Son, in Whom I am well pleased* [Mt. 3, 17], and without the reality of the flesh, John would not bear witness, *Behold the Lamb of God, behold Him Who takes away the sins of the world.* [Jn. 1, 29] Without the power of the Word, there would not take place the recovery of the weakly and the revival of the dead; and without the reality of the flesh, He would not need food after fasting, nor sleep after weariness. Lastly, without the power of the Word, the Lord would not declare Himself equal to the Father; and without the reality of the flesh the Selfsame would not call the Father greater than Himself, while the Catholic Faith accepts both statements and defends both, believing the one Son of God to be both Man and the Word, according to the distinctness of the Divine and human substance. Much is there, dearly beloved, which we might take out of the whole body of the Scriptures in order to expound this faith which we preach: for nothing is oftener presented to us in the Divine oracles, than the Son of God, as touching His Godhead, everlasting from the Father, and the Selfsame, as touching the flesh, born in time from His Mother.

ST. LEO THE GREAT [48]

Jesus appears in the world without giving any warning of his coming and without making known to any neighbour who he is.

Had he come into the world in his house at Nazareth, all his relatives would have made an event of his birth with the neighbours and the other inhabitants of the town. He would have been heralded and celebrated. He would thus have allowed himself to behave well enough like a true little Nazarene, but he would have been confiscated, as it were, by his earthly family and his earthly country. Quite to the contrary, he elects to be born away from home, on a journey, amid an anonymous crowd; in this way, he would really belong to everybody, and could come quietly and discreetly, with no tumult and excitement. God, if he had so wished, could naturally have made all sorts of efforts to spread the news abroad. And if any proof were needed of this, one could point to his having mobilized the angels but contented himself with bringing a few poor shepherds to the manger. It is also clear from this that he could easily have brought the whole of Jerusalem and all the just among the Israelites with pure and upright hearts, worshippers of God and living in expectancy of the Messias. And there were in fact many of them, all true friends of his, in the country of Judea and Galilee! But it is obvious that God did not wish to impose his Son: people must come to him by seeking and discovering him. Even the shepherds and the Wise Men, though warned personally, had to search for him with the help of a sign which, rather than leading them easily and directly to the manger, was little more than a suggestion to send them on their way. The shepherds must have gone to many houses and stables before they found the right babe wrapped in swaddling clothes. As for the Magi, they had to show some initiative in order to discover, by the normal means at their disposal, the birthplace of the young king of Israel. Jesus was infinitely discreet; he simply waited, and such a way of appearing could have made us somewhat impatient, had it not been proved for centuries back that men have found in this very discretion a true sign of God. That sign of weakness which draws men in spite of themselves, makes them surrender and acknowledge themselves outdone, without Jesus ever having forced himself upon them in any way other than a certain presence—a presence that waits, and invites, and demonstrates God's heaven in a humble manner which gives hope and humility, peace and love—just how, one does not really know! God is a master who knows how to go about speaking to us with the use of the things of earth—these various beings, both animate and inanimate—and the events of men's history.

RENE VOILLAUME [49]

THE HOLY NAME OF JESUS [1]

Jesus is Honey in the mouth, Music in the ear, a Song of gladness in the heart.

ST. BERNARD CLAIRVAUX [50]

JESU DULCIS MEMORIA

JESUS to cast one thought upon
Makes gladness after He is gone,
But more than honey and honeycomb
Is to come near and take Him home.

Song never was so sweet in ear,
Word never was such news to hear,
Thought half so sweet there is not one
As Jesus God the Father's Son.

Jesu, their hope who go astray,
So kind to those who ask the way,
So good to those who look for Thee,
To those who find what must Thou be?

To speak of that no tongue will do
Nor letters suit to spell it true;
But they can guess who have tasted of
What Jesus is and what is love.

Jesu, a springing well Thou art,
Daylight to head and treat to heart,
And matched with Thee there's nothing glad
That can be wished or can be had.

[1] This feast is celebrated on the Sunday which occurs from January 2 to 5. If there is no Sunday on those days, it is celebrated on January 2.

Wish us good morning when we wake
And light us, Lord, with Thy day-break.
Beat from our brains the thicky night
And fill the world up with delight.

Be our delight, O Jesu, now
As by and by our prize art Thou,
And grant our glorying may be
World without end alone in Thee.

GERARD MANLEY HOPKINS 51

Time of Epiphany

THE EPIPHANY OF THE LORD

The three mysteries of Epiphany.

Today's feast uses three symbols for the divine attraction that draws man with gifts of grace—the star, the sacred river, and the water changed into wine. But they are only symbols, not the truth itself. For the star signifies the Child, the river signifies the Lord and the divine remission and forgiveness of sin, and the wedding feast signifies the coming of the Spirit for our salvation. Humanity is made to see that it is not only under the law that demands grace, but that it is also under the law of genuine and effective grace. Precisely where he most needs help man finds it because God has placed himself on an equal footing with us. We are not alone—we can face anything that befalls us. And more than that, we are capable of living effectively when everything in our world seems to be against us. Remember St. Paul said: *My grace is sufficient* [2 Cor. 12, 9]—and it was sufficient to such an extent that to this day the world still admits it. Another great man said: "God alone suffices"—and he did suffice for a life whose fruits the world is still reaping.

ALFRED DELP [52]

Magi come from the East to adore the Virgin's Child. Today we celebrate this event; we pay our respects and deliver a sermon in keeping with the feast. This day first shone resplendently for the Magi; its anniversary is renewed by us with a festal rejoicing. They were the first-fruits of the Gentiles; we are a nation of Gentiles. The words of Apostles announced His birth to us; a star was, as it were, the language of heaven for them; like the heavens, therefore, the Apostles announced the glory of God to us. Why should we not recognize as heavens those who have become the abode of God, as it is written: *The soul of the just is the seat of wisdom?* [Wis. 7] For, through these heavens [the Apostles], the One who made and who dwells in the heavens has sounded forth. The earth trembled at the sound and now, behold, it believes. O mighty mystery! The Lord lay in a manger, yet He drew the Magi from the East. He was hidden in a stable, yet He was acknowledged in the heavens, so that, thus recognized in the heavens, He might be manifested in the stable and that this day might be called the Epiphany or, in the Latin derivative, the Manifestation. Thus, at one and the same time, He set His seal of approval on His high and His lowly estate, so that He to whom the heavens bore witness by a starry sign might, when sought, be found in an insignificant dwelling where, helpless in His tiny frame and wrapped in swaddling clothes, He might be adored by the Magi and feared by the wicked. . . .

Now, then, my dearly beloved sons and heirs of grace, look to your vocation and, since Christ has been revealed to both Jews and Gentiles as the cornerstone, cling together with most constant affection. For He was manifested in the very cradle of His infancy to those who were near and to those who were afar—to the Jews whose shepherds were nearby; to the Gentiles whose Magi were at a great distance. The former came to Him on the very day of His birth; the latter are believed to have come on this day. He was not revealed, therefore, to the shepherds because they were learned, nor to the Magi because they were righteous, for ignorance abounds in the rusticity of shepherds and impiety amid the sacrileges of the Magi. He, the cornerstone, joined both groups to Himself since He came to choose the foolish things of the world in order to put to shame the wise and *to call sinners, not the just* [Mt. 9, 13], so that the mighty would not be lifted up nor the lowly be in despair.

ST. AUGUSTINE [53]

Why cruel Herod vainly fear that Christ the Savior comes now here? (Vesper Hymn)

When we have thoughtfully looked at these points of comparison, dearly beloved, we find that Herod's character also is not absent. For the devil himself, as he was then Herod's secret instigator, so is now too his unwearied imitator. For he is tortured by the calling of all Gentiles, and agonized by the daily destruction of his own power; grieving that he is everywhere forsaken, and the true King in all places adored. He prepares deceits, he feigns agreements, he breaks forth into slaughter; and in order to make use of that remnant of men whom he still deceives, he burns with envy in Jews, he plots by craft in heretics, he is kindled with ferocity in Pagans. For he sees how invincible is the power of the eternal King, Whose own death has extinguished the power of death; and therefore he has put in force his whole art of doing mischief against those who serve the true King, hardening some by their inflated pride in knowledge of the law, depriving others into a frenzy of persecution. But this madness of this Herod is being overcome and crushed by Him Who crowned even little ones with the glory of martyrdom, and infused into His faithful ones so unconquerable a love, that they are bold to say in the Apostle's words, *Who shall separate us from the love of Christ? shall tribulation, or distress, or persecution, or famine, or nakedness, or peril, or sword? As it is written, For Your sake are we killed all the day long; we are counted as sheep for the slaughter. But in all these things we overcome by reason of Him that loved us.* [Rom. 8, 35–37]

ST. LEO THE GREAT [54]

THE EPIPHANY

To blaze the rising of this glorious sun
  A glittering star appeareth in the east,
Whose sight to pilgrim toils three sages won
  To seek the light they long had in request;
And by this star to nobler star they pass,
Whose arms did their desirèd sun embrace.

Stall was the sky wherein these planets shined,
  And want the cloud that did eclipse their rays;
Yet through this cloud their light did passage find,
  And pierced these sages' hearts by secret ways,
Which made them know the Ruler of the skies,
By infant's tongue and looks of babish eyes.

Heaven at her light, earth blusheth at her pride,
  And of their pomp these peers ashamèd be;
Their crowns, their robes, their trains they set aside,
  When God's poor cottage clouts and crew they see;
All glorious things their glory now despise,
Sith God contempt doth more than glory prize.

Three gifts they brought, three gifts they bear away;
  For incense, mirrh and gold, faith, hope and love;
And with their gifts the givers' hearts do stay,
  Their mind from Christ no parting can remove;
His humble state, his stall, his poor retinue,
They fancy more than all their rich revenue.

ROBERT SOUTHWELL [55]

FIRST SUNDAY AFTER EPIPHANY
THE HOLY FAMILY

In the name of the Lord Jesus. (Epistle)

The invocation of the name of Jesus seems, in the New Testament, to define the Christian. In view of the Old Testament invocation of the name of Yahweh, the invocation of the name of Jesus implies that Christians believed that Christ was God. But it does not imply that in their prayers Christ was simply substituted for Yahweh. The prayers themselves were addressed almost exclusively to the Father. "In the name of the Lord Jesus" meant not only pronouncing his name but also in union with him. Christians prayed always to the Father, in union with Christ Jesus, knowing that it was Christ who prayed in them, as their mediator. The expression, "in the name of Jesus," exhibits the originality of Christian prayer and manifests the Christian's realization of the Father's primacy in the work of salvation—in and through Christ.

STANISLAS LYONNET [56]

Clothe yourselves with love. (Epistle)

Do you take care of your wife as Christ takes care of the Church. Even if you must lay down your life for her, even if you must be cut into a thousand pieces, even if you must endure and suffer everything imaginable, do not refuse to do so; if you suffer these things, you have not yet done what Christ has done. You do them after you have already been joined to your bride; He did them for a bride who turned away from Him and hated Him. She turned from Him, hated Him, spat upon Him, and insulted Him, but He brought her into subjection by His own great solicitude and not by threats, nor insults, nor fear, nor anything of that sort. So you must take care of your wife; even if you see her despising you, insulting you, and scorning you, you will be able to bring her into subjection by your great care for her, by your love and friendship. Nothing is more tyrannical (in a good sense) than these bonds, and especially for a husband and wife. You might be able to bind a slave to you through fear; rather, you could not even bind a slave, because he would be quick to jump up and run away. But you must not bind by fear and threats your partner in life, the mother of your children, the foundation of all your joy; you must bind her to you by love and affection. What kind of union is it when the wife fears her husband? And what pleasure does he enjoy when he lives with his wife as if she were a slave and not a free woman? If you suffer anything in her behalf, do not revile her, for Christ did not do so. He delivered Himself up for her, that He might cleanse and sanctify her [see Eph. 5, 25–26].

ST. JOHN CHRYSOSTOM [57]

He went down to Nazareth and was subject unto them. (Gospel)

With its simplicity, Jesus' everyday life in and outside His family at Nazareth was the example of a perfect alliance between divine holiness and the human condition. Any man, whatever his situation or state in life, can therefore reach the perfection of Christian sanctity. However, Christian perfection, through the demands of faith and love, introduces into even the most ordinary life, the seeds of a veritable moral revolution.

If we wish to be Christians, we are bound to accept these seeds, with their possibilities of growth. . . .

The sternness one finds in the verses of the Gospel . . . may often give us pause. We may wonder just how far it is really possible to propose such an ideal of renunciation, faith, prayer and devotion in charity to laymen who are married or occupied in various ways. Yet all we are doing here is to indicate the logical consequences of Jesus' words as applied to any human life. It is a matter of pursuing an ideal, not of arriving before one has started. As has been said above, the call of Jesus takes us where we are and as we are on our journey to God. The ideal is so elevated that it may, indeed, seem inaccessible, but if one decides that it is not cut to one's measure, then one is consenting to mediocrity. It may be true that only a small number of men and women arrive at the perfection of the Gospel in this life; that, however, does not alter the fact that all are bound to strive towards it. Jesus never withdrew the order He gave men one day to be perfect as God the Father is perfect. Being a Christian does not necessarily mean to have achieved this ideal, but it certainly means to have striven, and to continue to strive, with perseverance and good will. True humility is required to be able to accept Our Lord's call in its absoluteness, while recognizing the imperfection of our lives with neither illusion nor discouragement.

We are not to select those Gospel demands that may seem better adapted to our lives than others, and leave the rest aside. We must be ready to accept them all as and when we are asked to do so.

JESUS CARITAS DIRECTORY [58]

These apostolic letters of St. Peter—like those of St. Paul, for that matter, and like all sacred Scripture—ought to furnish spiritual nourishment for all the Catholics in the world. . . . Nowadays ignorance of it [Scripture] on the part of any self-respecting Catholic is truly unforgivable.

JOHN XXIII [59]

Jesus Christ is a God whom we approach without pride, and before whom we humble ourselves without despair.

BLAISE PASCAL [60]

JANUARY 13
THE BAPTISM OF THE LORD

Jesus, in being himself baptized, hallowed baptism. If the Son of God was baptized, who any longer can claim to be godly and yet think lightly of baptism? He was not baptized that he might receive pardon for his sins, for he knew no sin; but being without sin he was baptized to impart divine grace and dignity to those who are baptized. For just *as the children are partakers of flesh and blood, he also himself likewise took part* [Heb. 2, 14] with them, so that we, by partaking in his presence after the flesh, may also become partakers of his divine grace. Jesus was baptized for that reason further also, that besides salvation, and through our partaking with him, we may receive the dignity. The dragon in the waters, according to Job, *trusteth that he can draw up Jordan into his mouth.* [40, 23] When, then, Jesus must break *the heads of the dragons* [Ps. 74, 14], he went down and bound the mighty one in the waters, so that we might receive the *power to tread upon serpents and scorpions.* [Lk. 10, 19] The beast was no ordinary monster, but a dread one. *No ship of fishers could bear one scale of his tail: before him ran destruction* [Job 40, 26], that laid waste all it met. But life ran to meet him, to muzzle death henceforth, that all we, the saved, may cry, *O death, where is thy sting? O grave, where is thy victory?* [1 Cor. 15, 55] Baptism destroys the sting of death. . . .

Jesus Christ was Son of God, but he did not preach the gospel till he had been baptized. Now if the Master himself pursued his course in regular order, ought we his servants to venture before the proper time? From that moment when *the Holy Spirit descended in a bodily shape like a dove upon him* [Lk. 3, 22] *began Jesus to preach.* [Mt. 4, 17] This was not so that Jesus should, for the first time, behold the Spirit, for he knew him before coming to earth in the body, but that John the Baptist should behold it. For said John, as I would have you note, *I knew him not; but he who sent me to baptize with water, the same said unto me, Upon whom you shall see the Spirit descending, and remaining upon him, the same is he.* [Jn. 1, 33] And if you have a sincere devotion, the Holy Spirit will descend also upon you, and the Father's voice will sound forth from on high: not to say "This is my Son," but to say "This is now become my son." "Is my Son" was said over him only, since *In the beginning was the Word, and the Word was with God, and the Word was God.* [Jn. 1, 1] To him applies the "is," since he is always Son of God, but to you applies the phrase "is now become," since you have not natural sonship, but receive the status of son by adoption. The Word is Son eternally. You receive the grace of sonship progressively. Therefore, to be made son of God, *an heir of God, and joint heir with Christ* [Rom. 8, 17], make ready the soul's vessel.

ST. CYRIL OF JERUSALEM [61]

When the Forerunner saw him who is our Illumination, who illuminates every man, coming to be baptized, his soul rejoiced, and his hand trembled. Then, pointing to him he said to the people, Behold the Rescuer of Israel, who delivers us from corruption. Wherefore, O Christ our God, who are sinless; glory to you.

The hosts of the angels trembled when they beheld our Redeemer being baptized by a servant, and testified to by the presence of the Spirit, while a heavenly voice from the Father cried, saying, Verily, this One on whom the Forerunner places his hands, is my beloved Son in whom I am well pleased. Wherefore, O Christ our God, glory to you.

The courses of the Jordan received you, O Fountain; and the Comforter descended in the likeness of a dove. Yea, he who bowed the heavens, bowed his own head; and the clay cried unto the potter, saying, How do you command me to do what is more exalted than my station? It is I who need to be baptized by you. Wherefore, O Christ God, who are sinless, glory to you.

When you chose to save lost man, you did not disdain to put on the likeness of a servant; for it was meet for you, O Lord God, to accept what is ours for our sakes; for when you were baptized in the flesh, O Redeemer, you made us worthy of forgiveness. Wherefore, we cry to you, O Christ our benevolent God, glory to you.

BYZANTINE LITURGY [62]

The mystery of the Baptism of Christ, the significance of which has hardly been examined by Western theology, has always held an important place with the Easterns. In it, they have seen one of the most complex and suggestive of mysteries and in that they are the inheritors of the most ancient tradition which, if we believe Peter's word about it in connexion with the election of Matthias [Acts 1, 22], made the Gospel story begin *from the time when John used to baptise*. Indeed, in its moderation, the scene is one of extraordinary power. The theophany at Jordan is the most perfect of Biblical theophanies: it reveals not only the inmost being of the Trinity, but also clearly foretells the reign of the Holy Ghost in the new life. Something is revealed here, too, regarding the redemptive sacrifice—a point that Jesus was to define more clearly later: *There is a baptism I must be baptised with.* [Lk. 12, 50]

The full significance of this feast was admirably summed up by the fourth-century writer Severus of Gabala:

> The adorable Trinity was present there, brilliantly manifesting his glory: the Father proclaiming his Son from on high, the Son here below fulfilling the economy of redemption, the Holy Ghost setting his seal upon the divine mystagogia. And the voice of the Father bearing his witness from heaven, was so powerful as to rend the skies.

CHARLES BURGARD [63]

EPIPHANY PREFACE

From the heavens over Jordan's bed the thunder rolled, telling us that you were there; it showed us the Saviour, who had come to us from heaven; it showed us you, the Father of the eternal Light.

You opened the heavens, blessed the air and cleansed the waters, and through the Holy Spirit, who appeared like a dove, you showed us your only Son.

This was the day when the waters received your blessing and took away the curse that had been laid on us. Now they can wash all sins away, if only men will believe; now they can make new children for God, adopting them to eternal life. Our birth in the flesh destined us to a life in time, our sin made us the prisoners of death; but now eternal life is open to us and we are called back to glory in the kingdom of heaven.

AMBROSIAN LITURGY [64]

Time after Epiphany to Septuagesima

The post-Epiphany season is a very elastic interval between Epiphany and Septuagesima, depending on the early or late date of Easter each year. Its last four Sundays have the same proper Mass chants, and instead of being used in January and early February the entire text of these Sundays is often used in the Fall to round out the number of Sundays after Pentecost. It would, consequently, seem unwise to try to discover any common theme among these six Sundays.

Nevertheless, without insisting on it too much, it seems possible to discover some common traits which will orient our usage of this season.

The first four Sundays appear in particular to be prolongations of the Epiphany mysteries. Jesus progressively reveals His nature and His mission so that at each stage men who are open to the divine and seeking God's will may discover Him to be Emmanuel.

First there is the revelation to the doctors of the old law and to His parents that He felt obliged to be about His Father's business. For all the blessed years of the hidden life at Nazareth, God had come to His temple to claim it as His own and had been recognized both implicitly and explicitly (see February 2) as its Lord.

On the second Sunday, Jesus *manifested his glory and his disciples believed in him* at Cana of Galilee. At the request of faith, He anticipates His "hour" and works a sign which brings to mind the ancient prophecies of the messianic age. Wine flows like water and the heavenly Bridegroom comes to claim His bride.

At Bethlehem, Jesus manifested himself to Jewish shepherds and to Gentile Magi. The Gospel of the third Sunday of Epiphany recounts a further revelation to a Jewish leper and to a Gentile centurion. Jesus marvels at the faith which makes miracles possible even for so-called unbelievers, and promises that on the basis of faith Jew and Gentile will gather together in the Kingdom of heaven.

The Gospel of the fourth Sunday reveals Christ's power over natural phenomena. He stills the winds and the sea, and His disciples, brought to a new level of faith, ask in amazement: *What kind of man is this?*

The final two Sundays may be thought of as Jesus' revelations of the kingdom of heaven. Both Gospels are from Matthew 13; the first speaks of the final messianic epiphany when Christ returns again in judgment to separate the weeds from the wheat; the second describes the growth and diffusion of the Church from her tiny origins at Bethlehem until the great assembly of men from every tribe and tongue and people and nation on the Last Day.

THE LORD HAS MADE KNOWN HIS SALVATION
[Psalm 97, 2]

SECOND SUNDAY AFTER EPIPHANY

Persevering in prayer. (Epistle)

Even though St. Paul tells Christians to pray without ceasing, and though to the Saints their very sleep is a prayer, there should be a regular fixed time for prayers, so that even if one is detained by work, the hour itself will remind you of your obligation. Hours of prayer, as everyone knows, are the third, sixth, and ninth hours, and at dawn and twilight. Prayers should always begin a meal, and never leave a table without first giving thanks to the Creator. Each night arise two or three times to meditate on those Scriptural passages you have memorized. Prayer should be your armor every time you step out of the house, and on returning, pray again before you are seated. The body should not have rest until the soul has been nourished. In everything Christians do, in every step they take, their hands should depict the sign of the cross.

ST. JEROME [65]

A wedding feast at Cana. (Gospel)

Christ's first miracle was performed at the celebration of an earthly union, at a wedding so joyous that the wine failed, and he had to change into wine the water in six stone jars intended for the ablutions.

He manifested his glory, writes John, *and his disciples believe in him.* [2, 11] It was then for their benefit he performed this act, to prepare them to reply to a second call by the complete gift of themselves. It was also because Mary had said to him, *They have no wine* [Jn. 2, 4], and despite his rather brusque words, he betrayed on this occasion a divine weakness in regard to his mother.

Already he had begun his habit of crossing every threshold, of sitting at every table; because it was for sinners he came, for those who were lost.

The scandal began at Cana, and lasted until Bethany, up to the time of the last anointing. The man who called himself the Son of God went every day among publicans, courtesans, the dissolute, the derelict. At Cana there were those who lived riotously and could not forego jests and laughter. The steward of the feast said to the bridegroom: *Every man sets forth good wine at first, and after they have drunk freely then that which is poorer; but you have kept the good wine until now.* [Jn. 2, 10] It is impossible to doubt that the contents of the six stone jars added to the joy of a wedding party already well filled with wine. More than one abstemious person put to Christ the hypocritical question which came up so often in the talk of the Pharisees: *Why do the disciples of John fast . . . while your disciples do not fast?* [Mk. 2, 18] But he smiled and was silent because his hour was not yet come.

Nevertheless, as he had been warned, Nathanael was the witness of a miracle more astonishing than that which had so amazed him at Bethany; what would the Son of Man not do thenceforth? The day he affirmed that wine was his blood and bread his flesh, those who had been at Cana would not be the last to believe. This first miracle, in appearance the least "spiritual" of all, prepared them for what was to come, introduced them to the unimaginable mystery.

FRANCOIS MAURIAC [66]

Mary and Eve.

As, in the imagery of Genesis, it is from the side of Adam that Eve is formed, and at his side that she stands as his helpmeet and the mother of men, so in John it is at the side of the crucified Christ that the second Eve stands, her compassion the helpmeet to his Passion, and from that position at his side that her second vocation, the motherhood of men *in vitam aeternam,* is inaugurated. Thus, for mother as for Son, Calvary is the culmination of what was initiated at Cana: the *beginning of the signs,* the *initia* of the messianic *mysterion,* is also the moment of separation (itself proclaimed beforehand in the synoptic losing-and-finding story of the Child in the temple) when the Word must leave mother and home behind him and embark on his journey as a homeless wanderer; and this is indicated by the title with which Jesus addressed his mother. The vocative *gynai,* "Woman," implies no disrespect, still less any rebuke: it expresses a formal courtesy; but for that very reason it is not a mode of address commonly used by son to mother, and in the Cana story it stands in sharp contrast to the immediately preceding phrase, "the mother of Jesus"; as Jesus, with the performing of his first sign, passes from the status of child to that of Son of Man, so Mary is formally addressed in terms of her vocation as second Eve, as Mother of Man, a role which in John 19, 26 is as it were formally promulgated.

GERALD VANN [67]

The "sign" of Cana has many facets to its mystery. Among other things Christians love to dwell upon it as a recognition and blessing of sacramental marriage.

How shall we ever be able adequately to describe the happiness of that marriage which the Church arranges, the Sacrifice strengthens, upon which the blessing sets a seal, at which angels are present as witnesses, and to which the Father gives His consent? For not even on earth do children marry properly and legally without their father's permission.

How beautiful, then, the marriage of two Christians, two who are one in hope, one in desire, one in the way of life they follow, one in the religion they practice. They are as brother and sister, both servants of the same Master. Nothing divides them, either in flesh or in spirit. They are, in very truth, two in one flesh; and where there is but one flesh there is also but one spirit. They pray together, they worship together, they fast together; instructing one another, encouraging one another, strengthening one another. Side by side they visit God's church and partake of God's Banquet; side by side they face difficulties and persecution, share their consolations. They have no secrets from one another; they never shun each other's company; they never bring sorrow to each other's hearts. Unembarrassed they visit the sick and assist the needy. They give alms without anxiety; they attend the Sacrifice without difficulty; they perform their daily exercises of piety without hindrance. They need not be furtive about making the Sign of the Cross, nor timorous in greeting the brethren, nor silent in asking a blessing of God. Psalms and hymns they sing to one another, striving to see which one of them will chant more beautifully the praises of their Lord. Hearing and seeing this, Christ rejoices. To such as these He gives His peace. Where there are two together, there also He is present; and where He is, there evil is not.

TERTULLIAN [68]

I have hitherto considered the cultivation of domestic affections as the source of more extended Christian love. Did time permit, I might now go on to show, besides, that they involve a real and difficult exercise of it. Nothing is more likely to engender selfish habits (which is the direct opposite and negation of charity), than independence in our worldly circumstances. Men who have no tie on them, who have no calls on their daily sympathy and tenderness, who have no one's comfort to consult, who can move about as they please, and indulge the love of variety and the restless humours which are so congenial to the minds of most men, are very unfavourably situated for obtaining that heavenly gift, which is described in our Liturgy, as being "the very bond of peace and of all virtues." On the other hand, I cannot fancy any state of life more favourable for the exercise of high Christian principle, and the matured and refined Christian spirit (that is, where the parties really seek to do their duty), than that of persons who differ in tastes and general character, being obliged by circumstances to live together, and mutually to accommodate to each other their respective wishes and pursuits. —And this is one among the many providential benefits (to those who will receive them) arising out of the Holy Estate of Matrimony; which not only calls out the tenderest and gentlest feelings of our nature, but, where persons do their duty, must be in various ways more or less a state of self-denial.

JOHN HENRY NEWMAN [69]

THIRD SUNDAY AFTER EPIPHANY

Be at peace with all men. . . . Do not avenge yourselves, (Epistle)

I think we *must first inquire whether warfare is proper at all for Christians.* What sense is there in discussing the merely accidental, when that on which it rests is to be condemned? Do we believe it lawful for a human oath to be superadded to one divine, and for a man to come under promise to another master after Christ, and to abjure father and mother and all nearest kinsfolk, whom even the law has commanded us to honour and love next to God Himself, to whom the gospel, too, holding them only of less account than Christ, has in like manner rendered honour? Shall it be held lawful to make an occupation of the sword, when the Lord proclaims that he who uses the sword shall perish by the sword? And shall the son of peace take part in the battle when it does not become him even to sue at law? And shall he apply the chain, and the prison, and the torture, and the punishment, who is not the avenger even of his own wrongs? Shall he either keep watch-service for others more than for Christ, or shall he do it on the Lord's day, when he does not even do it for Christ Himself? And shall he keep guard before the temples which he has renounced? And shall he take a meal where the apostle has forbidden him? And shall he diligently protect by night those whom in the daytime he has put to flight by his exorcisms, leaning and resting on the spear the while with which Christ's side was pierced? Shall he carry a flag, too, hostile to Christ? And shall *he* ask a watch-word from the emperor who has already received one from God? Shall *he* be disturbed in death by the trumpet of the trumpeter, who expects to be aroused by the angel's trump? And shall the Christian be burned according to camp rule, when he was not permitted to burn incense to an idol, when to him Christ remitted the punishment of fire? Then how many other offences there are involved in the performance of camp offices, which we must hold to involve a transgression of God's law, you may see by a slight survey. The very carrying of the name over from the camp of light to the camp of darkness is a violation of it. Of course, if faith comes later, and finds any preoccupied with military service, their case is different, as in the instance of those whom John used to receive for baptism, and of those most faithful centurions, I mean the centurion whom Christ approves, and the centurion whom Peter instructs; yet, at the same time, when a man has become a believer, and faith has been sealed, there must be either an immediate abandonment of it, which has been the course with many; or all sorts of quibbling will have to be resorted to in order to avoid offending God, and that is not allowed even outside of military service; or, last of all, for God the fate must be endured which a citizen-faith has been no less ready to accept. For neither does military service hold out escape from punishment of sins, or exemption from martyrdom. Nowhere does the Christian change his character. There is one gospel, and the same Jesus, who will one day deny every one who denies, and acknowledge every one who acknowledges God, —who will save, too, the life which has been lost for His sake; but, on the other hand, destroy that which for gain has been saved to His dishonour. With Him the faithful citizen is a soldier, just as the faithful soldier is a citizen. A state of faith admits no plea of necessity; they are under no necessity to sin, whose one necessity is, that they do not sin. For if one is pressed to the offering of sacrifice and the sheer denial of Christ by the necessity of torture or of punishment, yet discipline does not connive even at that necessity; because there is a higher necessity to dread denying and to undergo martyrdom, than to escape from suffering, and to render the homage required. In fact, an excuse of this sort overturns the entire essence of our sacrament, removing even the obstacle to voluntary sins; for it will be possible also to maintain that inclination is a necessity, as involving in it, a sort of compulsion.

TERTULLIAN [70]

Lord, I am not worthy! (Gospel)

What can I say to you, my God, but that I am a sinner? But you know that better than I and I would certainly neither believe nor admit it, if your word did not testify against me. Lord, do not depart from me, for I am a sinful man. Surely it is better to make this my appeal? Where, if not with you, could I take refuge in my weakness, in my spiritual sloth, in the duplicity and unreliability even of what is best in me? God of sinners, God of the habitual, daily, cowardly sinner, of the ordinary sinner! O God, there is nothing grand about my sin; it is so everyday, so normal, so much the accepted thing, that I can easily overlook it—only of course, when I overlook you, Most Holy One, and when I forget that you love us with a jealous love and want to possess our hearts, whole and undivided, burning and ready for anything. O God, whither could I flee? The great sinners could perhaps sate themselves for a time with the diabolical enormity of their sins. But what disgust I feel for my wretchedness, my complacent slowness of heart, the frightening mediocrity of my "good conscience." Only you could continue to tolerate such a heart, only you could continue to love me so patiently. You alone are greater than my poor heart. God of sinners, God even of the lukewarm and the slow of heart, have mercy on me.

KARL RAHNER [71]

Once again, as at Cana, Jesus manifests the glory of his divinity and messianic power and so leads men to belief.

What are these healings to Christ? Modernity, with its vital social and caritative sense, has tried to define the Lord as the great philanthropist, the friend of mankind who saw and helped its sufferings wherever possible. But modernity is oversimplifying. Love, yes; and deepest sympathy—his heart overflows with them. Even the Gospels, usually so reticent about feeling, frequently refer to these: *And when he landed, Jesus saw a large crowd, and had compassion on them, because they were like sheep without a shepherd. And he began to teach them many things.* [Mk. 6, 34] Yet Jesus is not merely a great figure of charity with a boundless heart and tremendous capacity for service. He makes no attempt to track human suffering to the root in order to eradicate it. He is no social reformer fighting for a more just distribution of material wealth. The social reformer aims at lessening suffering; if possible at removing it. He tries to meet human needs in a practical manner: to prevent misfortune, to readjust conditions in order that happy, physically and spiritually healthy people inhabit the earth. Once we see this clearly, we realize that for Jesus the problem is quite a different one. He sees the mystery of suffering much more profoundly—deep at the root-tip of human existence, and inseparable from sin and estrangement from God. He knows it to be the door in the soul that leads to God, or that at least can lead to him; result of sin but also means of purification and return. This is obviously what is meant by his words about taking up the cross and following him. [Mt. 16, 24] Perhaps we come nearer the truth when we say: Christ did not avoid pain, as we try to. He did not ignore it. He did not insulate himself from it. He received it into his heart. Sufferer himself and realist, he took people as he found them, with all their shortcomings. Voluntarily he shared their afflictions, their blame, their need. Herein lies the immeasurable depth and breadth of Christ's love. Its power is the triumphant power of truth in a love which seizes reality and lifts it out of itself. Jesus' healing is divine healing; it reveals the Universal Healer and directs towards him. It is inseparable from faith. In Nazareth he is unable to work miracles because the people there do not believe. To force the supernatural upon them would be to destroy its intrinsic sense: the faith from which it springs. The disciples are unable to cure the sick boy because they are faint-hearted, and the strength which should operate from the Holy Spirit is thus fettered. [Mt. 17, 14–21] When the paralytic is first brought to Jesus his physical disorder is apparently ignored. Before all else Jesus sees the sufferer's faith. Responding to this faith, the Lord forgives his sins; then, almost as a finishing touch, he cures him. To the father of the sick boy who begs Jesus: *But if you can do anything, have compassion on us and help us, Jesus replies: If you can believe, all things are possible to him who believes, and the miracle is performed.* [Mk. 9; 23–25]

Then we have the captain who confronts Jesus with military simplicity: *Lord, I am not worthy that you should come under my roof; but only say the word, and my servant shall be healed. . . . Go your way, Jesus answered; as you have believed, so be it done to you. And the servant was healed in that hour.* [Mt. 8, 5–13]

ROMANO GUARDINI [72]

FOURTH SUNDAY AFTER EPIPHANY

Love, therefore, is the fulfillment of the law. (Epistle)

Love, therefore, is the fulfillment of the law. [Rom. 13, 10] Charity is not just one commandment among the rest of the commandments nor one virtue among other virtues, but *the bond of perfection.* [Col. 3, 14] Without charity, life becomes meaningless and valueless for eternal life. Charity imparts true splendor to all things. An adequate comprehension of charity requires the fervor of the Seraphim. Natural man is incapable of grasping the full depths of divine charity. God Himself had to enunciate His personal charity to us. He sent His angels and prophets as messengers and as solicitors for our reciprocal love. Even more than this, the consubstantial Word of the Father became incarnate. We have seen the glory of the only-begotten Son of the Father full of grace and truth [see Jn. 1, 14]. Christ's salvific deeds and words revealed the inexhaustible treasures of divine love intended to enkindle the whole earth [see Lk. 12, 49]. The tongues of charity are more eloquent than those of angels. The fire of charity does not enkindle only the heavenly spirits with the ardor of divine love. Even we, poor mortals, may *comprehend what is the breadth and length and height and depth of the love of Christ which surpasses knowledge, in order that we may be filled unto all the fulness of God.* [Eph. 3, 18–19] The fire of God's charity, the Holy Spirit, will establish us firmly in charity in the consummation of perfect union with Christ.

BERNARD HARING [73]

Lord, save us! We are perishing! (Gospel)

Kristin woke up fully again with a start, and fixed her eyes upon her hand. The gold ring was gone, that was sure enough—but there was a white, worn mark where it had been on her middle finger. It showed forth quite clearly on the rough brown flesh—like a scar of thin, white skin—she deemed she could make out two round spots on either side where the rubies had been, and somewhat like a little mark, an M, where the middle plate of gold had been pierced with the first letter of Mary Virgin's holy name.

And the last clear thought that formed in her brain was that she should die ere this mark had time to vanish—and she was glad. It seemed to her to be a mystery that she could not fathom, but which she knew most surely none the less, that God had held her fast in a covenant made for her without her knowledge by a love poured on her richly—and in despite of her self-will, in despite of her heavy, earthbound spirit, somewhat of this love had become *part* of her, had wrought in her like sunlight in the earth, had brought fourth increase which not even the hottest flames of fleshly love nor its wildest bursts of wrath could lay waste wholly. A handmaiden of God had she been—a wayward, unruly servant, slothful and neglectful, impatient with correction, but little constant in her deeds—yet had he held her fast in his service, and under the glittering golden ring a mark had been set secretly upon her, showing that she was His handmaid, owned by the Lord and King who was now coming, borne by the priest's anointed hands, to give her freedom and salvation—

SIGRID UNDSET [74]

What manner of man is this? (Gospel)

See now the courtesy and mercy of Jesus. You have lost Him. But where? In your own house; that is, in your soul. If you had lost Him outside your own house—that is, if you had lost the power of reason through original sin—you would never have found Him again. But He left you your reason, and so He is within your soul, and will never be lost outside it. Nevertheless you are no nearer to Him until you have found Him. He is within you, although He is lost to you; but you are not in Him until you have found Him. In this, too, is His mercy, that He would suffer Himself to be lost only where He may be found. There is no need to travel to Rome or Jerusalem to search for Him: but turn your thoughts into your own soul where He is hidden, and seek Him there. For as the prophet says: *Truly, Lord, You are a hidden God.* [Is. 14, 15] And Christ himself says in the Gospel: *The kingdom of heaven is like a treasure hidden in a field, which when a man finds, for joy of it he goes and sells all that he has and buys that field.* [Mt. 13, 44] Jesus is the treasure hidden in your soul. If you could find Him in your soul, and your soul in Him, I am sure that you would gladly give up the love of all earthly things in order to have Him. Jesus sleeps spiritually in your heart as he once slept bodily in the ship with His disciples. But they, fearing to perish, awoke Him, and He quickly saved them from the tempest. Therefore rouse Him as they did by prayer, and wake Him with the loud cry of your desire, and He will quickly rise and help you.

WALTER HILTON [75]

FIFTH SUNDAY AFTER EPIPHANY

Whatever you do in word or in deed, do all in the name of the Lord Jesus. (Epistle)

At every forward step and movement, at every going in and out, when we put on our clothes and shoes, when we bathe, when we sit at table, when we light the lamps, on couch, on seat, in all the ordinary actions of daily life, we trace upon the forehead the sign [of the cross].

TERTULLIAN [76]

The marks of a true Christian.

Let no one deceive or lead another person astray, for, unless a man has been just, he does not have life in him; unless he has observed the commandments of Christ in every respect, he cannot have part with Him; unless he has despised earthly possessions, he will not gain heavenly ones; unless he has scorned human considerations, he will not have divine blessings. Let no one decide that he is a Christian unless he both follows the teaching of Christ and imitates His example. Do you think that man is a Christian who nourishes no needy person with his bread, who refreshes no thirsty person with his wine, whose table no one shares, under whose roof no stranger or wayfarer abides, whose garments clothe no naked person, whose helping hand assists no pauper, whose blessings no one experiences, whose mercy no one feels, who imitates the good in no way but rather laughs and mocks and persistently harasses the poor? Far be such an attitude from the minds of all Christians, far be it that any person of this sort be termed a Christian, far be it that such a one should be called the child of God. He is a Christian who follows the way of Christ, who imitates Christ in all things, as is written: *He who says that he abides in Christ ought himself to walk just as he walked.* [1 Jn. 2, 6] He is a Christian who shows mercy to all, who is not disturbed by any injury, who does not permit the poor to be oppressed in his presence, who assists the wretched and who succors the needy, who sympathizes with the sorrowful and who feels the grief of another as his own, who is reduced to tears by the weeping of another, whose house is common property for all, whose door is never closed to anyone, whose table is shared by every poor person, whose food is offered to all, whose goods all share and no one feels slighted, who serves God day and night, who meditates upon and considers His precepts ceaselessly, who makes himself poor in this world so that he may become rich in the eyes of God, who suffers himself to be considered of no account among men so that he may be acceptable before God and the angels, who seems to hold nothing concealed in his heart, whose soul is simple and spotless, whose conscience is faithful and pure, whose whole thought is directed to God and whose whole hope is in Christ, who desires heavenly rather than earthly possessions, who contemns earthly goods so that he may acquire divine. As for those who love this world and who are content and well pleased with this life, hear what the Scripture says to them: *Do you not know that the friendship of this world is enmity with God? Therefore, whoever wishes to be a friend of this world becomes an enemy of God.* [Jas. 4, 4]

ST. AUGUSTINE [77]

Let them both grow together until the harvest. (Gospel)

There is today, in this age, a terrestrial kingdom where dwells also the celestial kingdom. Each kingdom—the terrestrial kingdom and the celestial, the kingdom to be rooted up and that to be planted for eternity—has its various citizens. Only in this world the citizens of each kingdom are mingled; the body of the terrestrial kingdom and the body of the celestial kingdom are commingled. The celestial kingdom groans amid the citizens of the terrestrial kingdom, and sometimes (for this too must not be hushed) the terrestrial kingdom in some manner exacts service from the citizens of the kingdom of heaven, and the kingdom of heaven exacts service from the citizens of the terrestrial kingdom.

ST. AUGUSTINE [78]

The sinner and the saint are two essential and mutually complementary components which work upon one another; in their articulation is contained the whole secret of Christianity.

CHARLES PEGUY [79]

Still more palpable and painful does the conflict between the power of God and the weakness of man become when the instreaming life of grace and truth is checked by human passions, by sin and vice, when Christ as He is realized in human history is dragged through the dust of the street, through the commonplace and the trivial, and over masses of rubbish. That is the deepest tragedy, the very tragedy of the Divine, when It is dispensed by unworthy hands and received by unworthy lips. An immoral laity, bad priests, bishops and popes—these are the saddest wounds of the Body of the mystical Christ. This is what grieves the earnest Catholic and inspires his sorrowful lamentation, when he sees these wounds and is unable to help. "The Church," says Cardinal Newman, "is ever ailing, and lingers on in weakness, *always bearing about in the body the dying of the Lord Jesus, that the life also of Jesus might be made manifest in her body."* [2 Cor. 4, 10] It is an essential property of the Church to be so, because of her vocation to save men. Nowhere else does evil become so visible, because nowhere else is it so keenly fought. "She can never work out of the sphere of evil." As her Master came not for the whole, but for the sick, so the Church in this world will always have her sick, will always have sores in her members, great and small.

KARL ADAM [80]

Such is the composition of the Church, a mixture of the strong and the weak, the good and the bad, of hypocritical sinners and of scandalous sinners: the unity of the Church encloses them all and profits from them all. The faithful see on the one hand all that should be imitated and on the other what has to be surpassed courageously, reproved vigorously, supported patiently, helped charitably, heard compassionately, and watched with fear and trembling. Both those who remain and those who fall away equally serve the Church: the faithful, seeing conviction in the former and laxity in the latter, are astonished, edified, confounded, and encouraged in all instances, both because of the loving kindness and the justice of God. God must be adored in his unfathomable ways. All things work together for the salvation of those who love, even the cooling off, the defects and the cowardly want of love. Let him who understands, understand; and let him who has ears, hear. God opens the ears of those whom he pleases, but one must be faithful to him; woe to those who are not!

JACQUES BOSSUET [81]

SIXTH SUNDAY AFTER EPIPHANY

The kingdom of heaven is like a grain of mustard seed. (Gospel)

In the history of religion there have been two revolutions, called the two Testaments or, by St. Paul, "tremors of the earth." In the first man passed from idolatry to the Law, and in the second from the Law to the Gospel. And now we proclaim a third cataclysm, the transference from the present order to that beyond, where there can be no further change or disturbance.

One element the two Testaments have in common. They were established without any abrupt or instantaneous transformation.

It is well to realize the reason for this. God did not wish us to be coerced, but persuaded. For that which is not voluntary is not enduring, as we may see by comparison with the forceful repression of a stream or a plant. On the other hand, a transformation undertaken voluntarily is more lasting, more surely grounded. Coercion is the work of an external and tyrannical power, but choice is our own and is consonant with the goodness of God.

God, then, did not desire us to conform to the good under compulsion, but to choose the good. Hence, in the manner of one instructing children or tending the sick, he withdrew some of our traditional practices while condoning others, yielding to us on some small point to keep us happy. For it is not easy to abandon customs which long usage has invested with dignity and veneration.

Thus, the first Testament abolished idols, but allowed the traditional sacrifices; the second suppressed these, but did not forbid circumcision. In this way men accepted the suppression and then came to give up of their own accord what had been condoned—sacrifices under the old law, circumcision in the new. From pagans they became Jews, from Jews Christians, led furtively, one might say, towards the Gospel by these gradual changes.

With this process I may compare the development of the notion of the Godhead, except that here the process is reversed. In the former instance transformation came by way of suppression; but here perfection was approached by gradual increment. . . . This is what I mean.

The Old Testament unambiguously proclaimed the Father, the Son more obscurely; the New Testament gave full revelation of the Son, but put forward more tentatively the divinity of the Holy Ghost. But today the Holy Spirit is resident and active in our midst, giving us a clearer manifestation of his nature.

For it would have been misleading to proclaim decisively the divinity of the Son at a time when that of the Father was not openly admitted, or to add that of the Holy Ghost before the Son had been fully recognized, as an additional burden to our intellects, if I may use so bold an expression. We might, as children given food beyond their power of assimilation or as men of weak sight turning their gaze upon the sun, have imperilled what here and now lay within our grasp. It was more fitting that by piecemeal additions and, in the words of David, by gradual advance from splendour to splendour, the full radiance of the Trinity should come to shine on us.

ST. GREGORY NAZIANZEN [82]

When it grows up it is larger than any herb and becomes a tree. (Gospel)

Here is Christ Himself saying, as plainly as words can do it, that the kingdom of heaven will utterly change its appearance from being like a small, round seed, simple in shape and colour and texture, to the semblance of a vast, elaborate, glorious tree, of a thousand surfaces and curves, of innumerable branches, twigs, leaves, fibres and roots; from a seed which a bird can eat, to a tree in which a colony of birds may live.

Here is St. Paul, whom I now remember saying again and again that the Church is the *Body of Christ* [Eph. 2, 16], declaring that Body in his days to be as the body of a child, containing indeed the structure of an athlete, his limbs, his possibilities, but not actually expressing them; and that this Body will be gradually "edified" in the "unity"—not "diversity"—of "the faith, and of the knowledge of the Son of God," until it is full-grown—until it gradually corresponds in fact in its outward appearance and stature with the mind and spirit of Christ, which have been in it from the beginning! . . .

For I am more than the oak and the mustard-tree: I am the very Vine of God, *brought out of Egypt long ago.* [Ps. 79, 9] My seed fell in a ball of fire with the sound of wind; and from that moment I have lived indeed. I thrust my white shoots in the darkness of the catacombs, and forced my way through the cracks of Caesar's falling palaces; my early grapes were trodden under foot, rent by the wild boar in the amphitheatre, spoilt by little foxes, crushed in the wine-press of rack and prison; I am blown upon by every wind that blows, by calumny and criticism from the north, by passion and fury in the south and west. I am pruned year by year with sharp knives forged in death and hell, yet grasped by the hand of the Father who is my husbandman. And yet I live, and shall live, till my Beloved comes down to taste the fruits of the garden.

For I am planted by the river of salvation, watered by the tears and blood of saints, breathed upon by the spirit of God who alone can make the spices to flow forth. More than that, I am mystically one with my Beloved already; it is His Heart's blood that flows in my veins; His strength that sustains me; for He is the Vine, my boughs are His branches; and I am nothing save in Him and them. It is for this cause then that I spring up indomitable; that I stretch my boughs to the river, and my branches to the sea, that my shadow is in all lands; that the wild birds lodge in my branches, the dove and the eagle together; that the fierce beasts couch beside my roots, *the wolf beside the lamb, and the leopard by the kid.* [Is. 11, 6] It is for this that I am older than the centuries, younger than yesterday, eternal, undying and divine.

ROBERT BENSON [83]

The breakers of death surged round about me,
the destroying floods overwhelmed me;
The cords of the nether world enmeshed me,
the snares of death overtook me.

In my distress I called upon the LORD
and cried out to my God;
From his temple he heard my voice,
and my cry to him reached his ears
(*Introit of Septuagesima*)

Time of Septuagesima

It will be puzzling to most people in our days that the Church does not start her cycle of Scripture reading on the First Sunday in Advent, but on Septuagesima Sunday. This custom goes back to a time when the Church did not yet have an ecclesiastical year different from the civil year. In ancient Rome, the beginning of the year was celebrated early in Spring when after the lull of the Winter, life and light were again on the ascendancy. The Old Testament shows that the Jews once followed the same custom by calling the month in which the Spring feast of the Passover is celebrated *the first month of the year.* [Ex. 12, 1] Many passages in the writings of the early Fathers and in the liturgy indicate that the Christians of old considered Easter the "First Day," as the "Head," of the year. Because Lent and the pre-Lenten season belong to Easter as a time of preparation, Septuagesima Sunday is really the day when for the first time we scent the Holy Spring of Easter in the air. That is the reason why the Church wants us to read the Book of Genesis now. She wants us to contemplate the beginnings of the world in the light of Christ who *has appeared at the end of the ages* [Heb. 9, 26] to redeem it, because it is the same Son of God through whom all things received their first being, and through whom they were reëstablished on Easter. The work of creation foreshadows the work of Redemption, because Christ is the Alpha and the Omega, the beginning and the end of history.[1]

[1]Damasus Winzen, *Pathways in Holy Scripture,* Bethlehem, Connecticut, Regina Laudis, n.d.

Because the Scripture readings in the Divine Office are all taken from Genesis, the three weeks of the pre-Lenten season review the great facts of Creation and the Fall, the corruption of mankind and the Flood, the call of Abraham and God's covenant-promises to him and to his offspring.

Overshadowed in fact more by the Fall and the Flood than by the promises of redemption, pre-Lent has a rather somber tone. All use of the paschal alleluja ceases as the Church contemplates the misery of the human condition, and the proper chants of the Masses of this season are dolorful and almost desperate in the intensity of their pleas for assistance.

In part this tone is explainable by the historical origins of Septuagesima and Sexagesima Sundays in particular. Composed in a period of great distress when the city of Rome was beset on every side by famine, disease, and war, they reflect the miseries of an age of chaos and disintegration. But one need not know the actual origin of the Mass propers in order to enter into their spirit of anguish and dismay. What period in our personal or collective history is without its anxieties and its sufferings? The barbarous twentieth century with its frightful tale of torture, mass murder, and destruction of human values has surely even more reason to chant the psalms of penance than the Church of the barbarian invasions.

Septuagesima contains a solemn warning: *Many are called but few are chosen* (Gospel); *with most of them God was not well pleased* (Epistle). Nevertheless, the Gospel of this Sunday in conjunction with the readings from Genesis is also a vivid reminder of God's plan of having us cooperate with Him in building a world of ordered beauty, a world whose primeval integrity was marred by a tragic fall, but whose destiny is still assured by reason of God's abiding love and merciful interventions. Origen and St. Gregory the Great discovered in the relays of workmen sent to work in the vineyard all the stages of salvation history.

Sexagesima Sunday takes up this theme of divine and human cooperation in the parable of God's creative and redeeming Word sown broadcast in the world. Those who listen and respond generously to God's Word become new Pauls (Epistle) who can glory in their weakness because they have experienced the rescuing power of God. Even though the chants of the Mass still convey the trouble and anxiety of wounded creatures, the paschal spirit of renewal and rejuvenation is already breaking through the clouds.

Quinquagesima Sunday still maintains a Septuagesima-like tone in its Entrance Psalm, but the rest of the Mass *cries out with joy to the Lord* (Tract). The Epistle is St. Paul's magnificent panegyric on Christian love which is the sum and substance of our vocation as God's people. The Gospel records the tragic yet glorious prophecy of the approaching passion but then immediately affirms *on the third day he will rise again.* In the story of the pleading blind man who cries out in faith to *Jesus, Son of David,* we have a wonderful image of the redeemed whose lives are flooded with insight and meaning because of their faith in the divine Physician.

SEPTUAGESIMA SUNDAY

Anyone taking part in a contest, abstains from all things. (Epistle)

True detachment means a mind as little moved by what befalls, by joy and sorrow, honour and disgrace, as a broad mountain by a gentle breeze. Such motionless detachment makes a man superlatively Godlike. For that God is God is due to his motionless detachment, and it is from his detachment that he gets his purity and his simplicity and his immutability. If then a man is going to be like God, so far as any creature can resemble God, it will be by detachment. This leads to purity and from purity to simplicity and from simplicity to immovability; and it is these three which constitute the likeness between man and God, which likeness is in grace, for it is grace which draws a man away from mortal things and purges him from things corruptible. I would have you know that to be empty of creatures is to be full of God and to be full of creatures is to be empty of God.

JOHN ECKHART [84]

I bring my body into subjection. (Epistle)

God created Lucifer and adorned him with many beautiful gifts and graces. But what did Lucifer do? He took satisfaction in himself, was pleased with himself, he wanted to be something. In the same instant in which he wanted to be something he became nothing and fell very low.

We find the same thing in our first parents, whom God also adorned with precious gifts and graces. The devil tempted Eve with a fruit. But she would not take it, because she did not want to die and become nothing. "No," the devil answered, "you will become something, you will be, *eritis*." This promise sounded so pleasant to her, rang so sweetly in the ears of her soul, and was so tempting to her, that she seized the forbidden fruit and tasted it. This was the undoing of all of us down to the last person to be born into this world, Eve's children and grandchildren. He who wants to become something, must be satisfied to be nothing.

This renunciation of self and willingness to be nothing is the basis and foundation of our holiness. He who wishes to become what he is not will end up no longer being what he is. This is a necessary consequence. God, the pure, lovable Good, is an unchangeable essence, an essential being, always remaining the same in himself. All creatures should exist for him and through him, not for themselves. He is the essence of all things [insofar as he is present to all things as the cause of their being].

Man must have a profound abandonment and renunciation of himself. How profound must this be? If a stone were to drop into a bottomless ocean, it would never stop sinking because the ocean had no bottom. Man must have a similar immersion and submersion in God's fathomless depths. He must be grounded in God, no matter what heavy trials come upon him, interiorly or exteriorly—sufferings caused by other people or by his own frailty, which God often permits to come upon him for his own good. This should make a man sink ever deeper into God without ever reaching the bottom, because there is no bottom. He should not complain nor fret, nor seek himself in anything. He should seek only God, in whom he is submerged. He who seeks anything else than God, does not truly seek God. Man's entire happiness should be to give glory to God and to fulfill his will at all times. He must never seek his own profit, exaltation, or reward. He must seek God alone and say with the Eternal Son: *I am not looking to my own reputation but to the Father's.* [Jn. 8, 49] He who acts contrary to this teaching is unjust and is committing error. No matter how beautiful a glass may be, it is not perfect if there is in it a hole the size of a pinpoint. No matter how small the flaw, it detracts from completeness and perfection.

HENRY SUSO [85]

God is the Lord of history, sending workers into his vineyard as his loving design demands.

Five ages of the world, accordingly, having been now completed (there has entered the sixth). Of these ages the first is from the beginning of the human race, that is, from Adam, who was the first man that was made, down to Noah, who constructed the ark at the time of the flood. Then the second extends from that period on to Abraham, who was called the father indeed of all nations which should follow the example of his faith, but who at the same time in the way of natural descent from his own flesh was the father of the destined people of the Jews; which people, previous to the entrance of the Gentiles into the Christian faith, was the one people among all the nations of all lands that worshipped the one true God: from which people also Christ the Saviour was decreed to come according to the flesh. For these turning points of those two ages occupy an eminent place in the ancient books. On the other hand, those of the other three ages are also declared in the Gospel, where the descent of the Lord Jesus Christ according to the flesh is likewise mentioned. For the third age extends from Abraham on to David the king; the fourth from David on to that captivity whereby the people of God passed into Babylonia; and the fifth from that transmigration down to the advent of our Lord Jesus Christ. With His coming the sixth age has entered on its process; so that now the spiritual grace, which in previous times was known to a few patriarchs and prophets, may be made manifest to all nations; to the intent that no man should worship God but freely, fondly desiring of Him not the visible rewards of His services and the happiness of this present life, but that eternal life alone in which he is to enjoy God himself: in order that in this sixth age the mind of man may be renewed after the image of God, even as on the sixth day man was made after the image of God. For then, too, is the law fulfilled, when all that it has commanded is done, not in the strong desire for things temporal, but in the love of Him who has given the commandment.

ST. AUGUSTINE [86]

Workers in the vineyard.

Observe in the parable the Master of the Vineyard did but one thing. He told his servant to *call the labourers and give them their hire*. He did but ask *what they had done*. He did not ask what their opinion was about science, or about art, or about the means of wealth, or about public affairs; he did not ask them if they knew the nature of the vine for which they had been labouring. They were not required to know how many kinds of vines there were in the world, and what countries vines could grow in, and where they could not. They were not called upon to give their opinion what soils were best for the vines. They were not examined in the minerals, or the shrubs, or in anything else which was found in the vineyard, but this was the sole question, whether they had *worked* in the vineyard. First they must be in the vineyard, then they must work in it; these were the two things. So will it be with us after death. When we come into God's presence, we shall be asked two things, whether we were in the Church, and whether we worked in the Church. Everything else is worthless. Whether we have been rich or poor, whether we have been learned or unlearned, whether we have been prosperous or afflicted, whether we have been sick or well, whether we have had a good name or a bad one, all this will be far from the work of that day. The single question will be, are we Catholics and are we good Catholics? If we have not been, it will avail nothing that we have been ever so honoured here, ever so successful, have had ever so good a name. And if we have been, it will matter nothing though we have been ever so despised, ever so poor, ever so hardly pressed, ever so troubled, ever so unfriended. Christ will make up everything to us, if we have been faithful to Him; and He will take everything away from us, if we have lived to the world.

Then will be fulfilled the awful words of the parable. Many that are last shall be first, *for many are called but few are chosen.* Then, also, will it be seen how many have received grace and have not profited by it. Then will be seen how many were called, called by the influence of God's grace, called into the Church, yet how few have a place prepared in heaven. Then will be seen how many resisted their conscience, resisted the call of Christ to follow Him, and so are lost. This is the day both of divine grace and of patience. God gives grace and is patient with us, but when death comes, there is no more time either for grace or for patience. Grace is exhausted, patience is exhausted. Nothing remains but judgement, a terrible judgement on those who have lived in disobedience.

And oh! what a sight it will be, what an unexpected sight, at the last day and public judgement to be present at that revelation of all hearts! How different persons will then seem, from what they seem now! How will the last be first, and the first last! Then those whom the world looked up to, will be brought low, and those who were little esteemed, will be exalted. Then will it be found who are the real movers in the world's affairs, those who sustained the cause of the Church or who influenced the fortunes of empires, were not the great and powerful, not those whose names are known in the world, but the humble despised followers of the Lamb, the meek saint, the man full of prayer and good works whom the world passed by; the hidden band of saintly witnesses, whose voice day by day ascended to Christ; the sufferers who seemed to be living for nothing; the poor whom the proud world thought but an offence and a nuisance.

JOHN HENRY NEWMAN [87]

SEXAGESIMA SUNDAY

In former times, the popes celebrated the Mass of this Sunday in the basilica and shrine-church of St. Paul Outside the Walls of Rome. Hence the allusion to the Apostle of the Gentiles in the Collect and the choice of the Epistle.

Paul possessed a power greater than that of preaching and capable of producing greater effects. For when he merely appeared, though he uttered not a word, he was an object of terror to the devils. Now all the men of the present day together could not accomplish by endless prayers and tears as much as the garments of Paul once accomplished. By prayer Paul raised the dead to life, and worked wonders so great that by those without he was taken for a god; and before he passed from this life he was deemed worthy to be elevated to the third heaven, and to hear words which it is not permitted to the nature of man to hear. . . . If we leave miracles out of the question and come to the life of that blessed man and examine his angelic conduct, we shall see the athlete of Christ excel in this respect even more than in miracles. Why mention his zeal, his modesty, his frequent perils, his constant cares, his incessant solicitude for the churches, his compassion for the poor, his many trials, his repeated persecutions, his daily deaths? For what spot in the world, what continent, what sea was not a witness of the contests of this just man? The desert knew him, for it received him often in his perils. He endured every form of attack and obtained every kind of victory, and never ceased to combat and to conquer. But I know not how I have been led on to insult the man, for his good deeds surpass all expression, and all that I can say, as far as the masters of eloquence surpass me. . . . After so many good works, after so many victories, he prayed that he might be cast into hell and consigned to everlasting punishment, that the Jews who had frequently stoned him, and, as far as in them lay, put him to death, might be saved and come to Christ. Who loved Christ so much as he, if indeed that must be called love, and not something greater than love? . . .

In what did that blessed man surpass the other apostles? Why is he spoken of throughout the whole world? Why is he most of all admired not only by us but also by Jews and Greeks? Is it not on account of the excellence of his epistles, by which he benefited not only the faithful who lived at that time, but also those who have lived from that time till now, and those who shall live until the final coming of Christ, and he shall never cease to do so as long as the human race exists? For his writings, like a wall of adamant, protect all the churches throughout the entire world. Even now he stands in our midst like a valiant athlete *bringing into captivity every understanding unto the obedience of Christ, and destroying counsels and every height that exalts itself against the knowledge of God.* [2 Cor. 10, 4, 5] All this he does by means of those admirable epistles, full of divine wisdom, which he has left us. And his writings are useful, not only to refute false doctrine and to defend that which is true, but they are also of no small utility to instruct us how to lead a good life. For even now by means of them the prelates of the Church deck and adorn and form to spiritual beauty the chaste Virgin whom he espoused to Christ. By these they ward off the diseases which attack her, and preserve her in health. Such remedies did that ignorant man leave us, possessing a power which they who frequently use them know by experience.

ST. JOHN CHRYSOSTOM [88]

Even so, the last shall be first, and the first last. (Gospel)

When he woke up it was dawn. He woke with a huge feeling of hope which suddenly and completely left him at the first sight of the prison yard. It was the morning of his death. He crouched on the floor with the empty brandy flask in his hand trying to remember an act of contrition. "O God, I am sorry and beg pardon for all my sins . . . crucified . . . worthy of Thy dreadful punishments." He was confused, his mind was on other things: it was not the good death for which one always prayed. He caught sight of his own shadow on the cell wall: it had a look of surprise and grotesque unimportance. What a fool he had been to think that he was strong enough when others fled. What an impossible fellow I am, he thought, and how useless. I have done nothing for anybody. I might just as well have never lived. His parents were dead—soon he wouldn't even be a memory—perhaps after all he wasn't really Hell-worthy. Tears poured down his face: he was not at the moment afraid of damnation—even the fear of pain was in the background. He felt only an immense disappointment because he had to go to God empty-handed, with nothing done at all. It seemed to him at that moment that it would have been quite easy to have been a saint. It would only have needed a little self-restraint and a little courage. He felt like someone who has missed happiness by seconds at an appointed place. He knew now that at the end there was only one thing that counted—to be a saint.

GRAHAM GREENE [89]

This failure of the soul to find objects and persons worthy of its love may lead to weary renunciation, to a hopelessness which drowns itself in pleasure-seeking, to a bitterness that turns against everything. But it may suddenly dawn on the seeker that what he is seeking must nevertheless exist. And it is not only more than the world can give, not only greater or better or more beautiful, but different; unknown and yet familiar, a mystery and yet divined; beyond things and men; on high.

Once this yearning of ours leaves material things behind and reaches out with a pure, searching longing, it has already attained to God. This kind of seeking means that the object of our searching has already been found, for it is the Living God himself who causes us to seek and uses our restless searching to draw us to himself.

In such yearning we become aware of God, even if it be only in the act of reaching out for Him. God is the object of our longing, and He will satisfy us.

ROMANO GUARDINI [90]

Poverty in the Church.

What is the meaning of poverty within the Church? No one can deny that it was chosen by the incarnate Son of God, who being rich, made himself poor. This choice he constantly maintained throughout his life, from the stable at Bethlehem to the nudity of the Cross. What is more, he preached poverty and held it forth as an inescapable demand for those who wished to be his disciples.

This seems to me to constitute above all the mystery of poverty in the Church; a mystery, moreover, which is bound up not only with its evangelical origins but its entire history. So much so that the great epochs, the great movements of internal reformation and renewal within the Church, and the periods of its most auspicious expansion throughout the world have invariably been those epochs in which the spirit of poverty has been affirmed and lived to the most manifest degree.

GIACOMO LERCARO [91]

QUINQUAGESIMA SUNDAY

The greatest of these is charity. (Epistle)

St. Paul bears witness that all exterior hardships, all mortifications of the flesh and all bodily labours are as nothing compared with love, which purifies the heart and makes it shine with light. *Bodily exercise is profitable to little: but godliness is profitable to all things* [1 Tim. 4, 8], that is, bodily effort avails little, but a sweet and pure heart avails to all things. *If I speak with the tongues of men and angels, etc; if I should deliver my body to be burned, etc; if I should distribute all my goods to feed the poor, and have not charity, it profiteth me nothing.* [1 Cor. 13, 1, 3] Even if I knew the languages of men and of angels, he says, even if I inflicted on my body all the torture and agony that the body could bear, even if I gave all I had to the poor; if I had not love also, towards God and towards all men, in Him and for Him, all would be lost, for as the holy abbot Moses said, "All the suffering and all the hardship that we suffer in the flesh, and all the good we ever do, all such things are but implements with which to cultivate the heart." If the axe did not cut, nor the pikestaff pierce the ground, nor the ploughshare plough, who would want to keep them? Just as no one cares for the implements for their own sake, but for the things which are done with them, so one should not value bodily suffering except for this reason, that God may the sooner turn towards it with His grace, and make the heart pure and clearsighted, and this no one may achieve who is tainted with vices or with an earthly love of worldly things, for this taint affects the eyes of the heart so badly that it cannot recognize God or rejoice in the sight of Him. A pure heart, as St. Bernard says, effects two things: it makes you do all that you do either for the love of God alone, or for the good of others for His sake. In all that you do, have one of these two intentions, or both together, for the second comes under the first. Always keep your heart pure in this way, and then do anything you will; have a confused heart, and all will be evil for you. *All things are clean to the clean, but to them that are defiled nothing is clean,* says the Apostle. [Tit. 1, 15] St. Augustine says, "Have charity, and do what you will, that is, by the will of reason."

ANCRENE RIWLE [92]

Those who suffer persecution for justice' sake. We know approximately, or we believe we know, what persecution is. But "for justice' sake"—there we feel the presence of a mystery. What is this justice for the sake of which they are persecuted?

The saints know what is this justice. They are persecuted for the sake of the justice which makes us adopted sons of God and participants in His life through grace; they are persecuted for the sake of the divine truth to which they bear witness and of that Word which was made flesh and came to dwell in the world and *His own received Him not* [Jn. 1, 11]; they are persecuted for the sake of Jesus Who is our justice. *Blessed are ye when they shall revile you and persecute you and speak all that is evil against you, untruly, for my sake: be glad and rejoice, for your reward is very great in heaven. For so they persecuted the prophets that were before you.* [Mt. 5, 11–12]

Blessed are the saints. They know wherefor they suffer. Not only do they suffer for justice' "sake" but "for" justice, which they know and which they love and which they will. Throughout their worst sufferings and their darkest nights they are well satisfied to be persecuted, they know that persecution is good for them, they desire it as they might desire an earthly paradise, they are astonished and worried when persecution is lacking to them. But never do they lack it long. Saint Paul reassures them and tells them that all those who seek to live piously in Christ Jesus will suffer persecution. When they are persecuted they have obtained that which they have wanted, they have that blessedness of the Gospel for which they have asked, they are well served.

JACQUES MARITAIN [93]

Lord, why did you tell me to love men, all my brothers?
I have tried but now I come back, frightened, to you . . .
Lord, I was so peaceful in my house, I had everything nicely arranged and I was quietly settled in.
My house was all furnished and everything seemed all right.
Alone, I was at peace with myself, sheltered from the wind, the rain and the mire.
I could have remained whole and intact, shut up in my tower.
But you found a crack in my defences, Lord:
You made me open my door just a bit,
And like a cloudburst full in the face, the cries of men awoke me;
Like a gust of wind, I was shaken by a friendship;
Like a ray of sun peeping unexpectedly between the shutters, your grace had disturbed me . . . and I left my door ajar, incautious that I was.
Now I am lost, Lord!

Outside men were watching for me.
I had not known they were so near; in that house, in that street, in that office—my neighbor, my colleague, my friend.
As soon as I started to open the door, I saw them there with their hands, their looks, their very souls stretching out, waiting like beggars outside a church.

The first of them came in, Lord—there was still a little room in my heart.
I let them come gladly, I would have cared for them, talked to them, cheered them, these sheep of mine, my own little flock.

You would have been pleased, Lord, well served, duly honoured —neatly and politely.
It was all quite reasonable up till then . . .
But those that followed, Lord—I had not seen those others; they had been hidden by the first ones.
There were more of these; they were more wretched, too, and they came streaming in without waiting to be asked.
We had to move up and make room for one another in my house.
And now they have come from everywhere, wave after wave of them, each new wave pushing and jostling the last.
They have come from everywhere, from every part of the city, from the entire country, from the whole world, uncountable, unending.
They no longer come singly, but in groups, in lines, as if mixed together, bound together, welded together like pieces of humanity.
They no longer come with empty hands but laden with heavy luggage—the luggage of injustice, of rancour and hate, the luggage of suffering and sin.
Behind them they trail the World, with all its tools, twisted and rusty or too new and ill-adjusted, wrongly used.

Lord, they are getting in my way, taking all the room, hurting me!
They are too hungry—they are devouring all I had and me myself.
I can do nothing any more; the more they pour in and the more they push at the door, the wider the door opens . . .

O Lord! My door is breaking down!
I can't go on! It is too much for me! Life is not worth this!
What about my position?
What about my family?
And my peace of mind?
And my freedom?
And what about me?
Ah! Lord! everything has been taken from me. I no longer even belong to myself.
There is no room for me in my own house.

*

Have no fear, says God, you have not lost all but gained all.
For while men were pouring into your house,
I, your Father,
I, your Lord,
Slipped in with them.

MICHEL QUOIST [94]

The street will be long and unfriendly, the stairs steep and the poor often ungrateful.

You will soon find charity a heavy burden, Jeanne, heavier than the jug of soup or the full basket. But you will still be pleasant and smile. Distributing soup and bread is not everything. The rich can do that. You are the little servant of the poor and the daughter of Charity, always smiling and good tempered. They are your masters and you will find them terribly exacting masters.

So the more unattractive and dirty they are, the more rude and unfair they are, the more you must lavish your love upon them. It is only by feeling your love that the poor will forgive you for your gifts of bread.

JEAN ANOUILH [95]

Communion with Christ calls for, and contains in embryo, communion with all men. Let us then tear down the walls which separate us. Let us strive to release in each of our erring brothers the imprisoned song which longs to rise up to God with ours. Are we to keep for ourselves this light which was revealed to us at no cost to ourselves? The only life which achieves fulfilment is the one which has been imparted to others, radiant and fruitful.

PAUL CLAUDEL [96]

Jesus prophesies his passion.

When the disciples shrank from His words about His own death and passion, what did He do? He met a blind man, and He took him and gave him sight. Why did He give him this special favour? He expressly tells us. He says, *your faith has made you whole*. [Lk. 18, 42] Here was a tacit rebuke of the slowness to believe in His own disciples and friends, all things are possible to him that believeth. This poor outcast is a lesson to you, O My own people. He puts you to shame. He has had faith in Me, while ye stumble at My word, and when I say a thing, answer *Be it far from You, Lord*. [Mt. 16, 22]

The office this day gives us another instance of the same great lesson. The Church reads today the history of the call of Abraham, and meditates upon his great act of obedience, in lifting up his knife to slay his son. Abraham, our father, is our great pattern of faith, and his faith was tried, first by being called on to leave his country and kindred, next by being told to sacrifice his dearly beloved Isaac. The first was trying enough, but what a stumbling-block the second might have been to faith less than his. If the disciples were shocked that the divine Antitype should be put to death, surely Abraham too had cause of offence that his own Isaac was to be struck down and slain by him, by his hand, by the hand of his father! Yet he went about the fulfilment of this command, as gravely, as quietly, as calmly, as if it was a mere ordinary action. Thus he showed his faith and gained the blessing.

Be sure, my Brethren, that this must be our way too. Never does God give faith, but He tries it, and none without faith can enter the kingdom of heaven. Therefore all ye who come to serve God, all ye who wish to save your souls, begin with making up your minds that you cannot do so, without a generous faith, a generous self-surrender; without putting yourselves into God's hands, making no bargain with Him, not stipulating conditions, but saying "O Lord here I am—I will be whatever Thou wilt ask me—I will go whithersoever Thou sendest me."

JOHN HENRY NEWMAN [97]

The mystery of God's plan.

Yet Abraham believed and did not doubt, he believed the preposterous. If Abraham had doubted—then he would have done something else, something glorious; for how could Abraham do anything but what is great and glorious! He would have marched up to Mount Moriah, he would have cleft the fire-wood, lit the pyre, drawn the knife—he would have cried out to God, "Despise not this sacrifice, it is not the best thing I possess, that I know well, for what is an old man in comparison with the child I promise; but it is the best I am able to give Thee. Let Isaac never come to know this, that he may console himself with his youth." He would have plunged the knife into his own breast. He would have been admired in the world, and his name would not have been forgotten; but it is one thing to be admired, and another to be the guiding star which saves the anguished.

SØREN KIERKEGAARD [98]

In the light of the Cross.

The Cross is therefore not inhuman but superhuman. We can now understand that from the very first, from the very origins of mankind as we know it, the Cross was placed on the crest of the road which leads to the highest peaks of creation. But, in the growing light of revelation, its arms, which at first were bare, show themselves to have put on Christ: *Crux inuncta.* At first sight the bleeding body may seem mournful to us. Is it not from the night that it shines forth? But if we go nearer we shall recognise the flaming Seraphim of Alvernus whose passion and compassion are *incendium mentis.* The Christian is not asked to swoon in the shadow, but to climb in the light, of the Cross.

PIERRE TEILHARD DE CHARDIN [99]

Sanctoral

We should imitate the virtues of the saints
just as they imitated Christ,
for in their virtues there shine forth
under different aspects
the virtues of the Divine Redeemer.
(Pius XII, *Mediator Dei*)

THE LOVE OF GOD

Nothing is inexorable but love. Love which will yield to prayer is imperfect and poor. Nor is it then the love that yields, but its alloy . . . For love loves unto purity. Love has ever in view the absolute loveliness of that which it beholds. Where loveliness is incomplete, and love cannot love its fill of loving, it spends itself to make more lovely, that it may love more; it strives for perfection, even that itself may be perfected—not in itself, but in the object . . . Therefore all that is not beautiful in the beloved, all that comes between and is not of love's kind, must be destroyed. And our God is a consuming fire.

GEORGE MACDONALD [100]

The Saints in Our Life

In addition to the great paschal cycle of salvation mysteries commemorated and re-enacted liturgically each year, the Church has another which crosses and recrosses the former's development continuously. The latter series of feasts—the sanctoral cycle—has no logical or historical link at all to make it an organic whole. Saints separated by centuries and by continents and by states of life appear side by side in the calendar in the most haphazard fashion.

In the past there often appeared to be a kind of liturgical rivalry between the two cycles. The peaceful and gradual invasion of the Church's year by the saints threatened to submerge the Lord's cycle. Although originally such feasts were celebrated annually only in chapels built over the tombs or relics of the martyrs or (after the fourth century) of other outstanding Christians, little by little their Mass and Office penetrated the Missal and Breviary of whole countries and even continents in such profusion that they threatened the entire primitive liturgical cycle and even the Lord's Day itself. Moreover, the growth of popular and literary legends about so many of the saints appeared to menace the primacy of biblical texts and biblical inspiration in the liturgy.

Both Catholic and Protestant reformers of the sixteenth century were concerned about cleansing the liturgical year of such unwarranted excrescences. Anglicans and Lutherans swept away many feasts of the saints in their zeal to restore the temporal cycle and to purify the sanctoral. After the Council of Trent, and the consequent centralization of liturgical authority in the Roman rite, Catholic liturgists were able to begin a more practical reform of the sanctoral cycle. Nevertheless, the work was always to be done again as more and more saints were canonized and only too often found their way into the calendar of the universal Church. Such was the liturgical drawback of sanctity! In the middle of the eighteenth century, Pope Benedict XIV prepared for a thorough purging of the sanctoral again, but died before his reforms could be instituted. St. Pius X saw some of these through early in this century and prepared the way for distinguished liturgists and latterday popes to undertake a serious reform. The Liturgical Constitution of Vatican Council II has laid down the following principle:

> Lest the feasts of the saints should take precedence over the feasts which commemorate the very mysteries of salvation, many of them should be left to be celebrated by a particular Church or nation or family of religious; only those should be extended to the universal Church which commemorate saints who are truly of universal importance.[1]

CHRIST'S EPIPHANY IN HIS SAINTS

The liturgical year is designed to make us progressively more like Christ by having us continuously relive His mysteries. It causes the actual growth of the incarnate Word in His totality of both Head and members, of the "whole Christ," [2] to use the expression of St. Augustine. Jesus cannot be considered apart from the members of His Mystical Body since they are the reason and purpose of His mission. By His passion He merited to be their risen Head and to diffuse His interior life in them until the end of time. He truly lives in His disciples: *It is now no longer I who live, but Christ lives in me.* [Gal. 2, 20] All that they do as disciples, He can claim as His own. Normally, it is through and in His members that Jesus reveals himself to men, practicing a kind of continuous epiphany of light and love in our mortal bodies. With real humility St. Paul could guarantee his followers that his witness to Christ was true: *By the grace of God I am*

[1] *Constitution on the Sacred Liturgy,* Chapter V, number 111.

[2] See the list of references in E. Mersch, *The Theology of the Mystical Body,* St. Louis, B. Herder, 1951, pp. 151–152.

what I am and his grace in me has not been fruitless . . . Be imitators of me as I am of Christ. [1 Cor. 15, 10; 4, 16] And all around him, in other disciples, Paul recognized and hailed the divine achievement, the *glory of Christ,* its true author. [2 Cor. 4, 7; 8, 23]

In the first age of the Church, Christians venerated not only the apostles (and later their descendants, the bishops), submitting to them as to Jesus Christ himself—whatever their personal qualities might be[3]—but also spontaneously reverenced the "true disciples" [4] whose union with Christ was so close as to be unmistakable in the minds of the faithful.

You shall be my witnesses. [Acts 1, 8] Such witnessing is more a matter of living than of speaking and at times culminates in dying for Christ's name. The latter witness we still call by his Greek name, *martyr*. The Acts of the Apostles in recounting the death of Stephen the Deacon, and the Christians of Smyrna in describing the martyrdom of their bishop Polycarp, wanted to bring out their resemblance to the Savior. The companions of Blandina saw Christ crucified accompanying the martyr as she hung suspended from a stake in the midst of the arena, and Ignatius of Antioch pleaded: "Let me imitate the suffering of my God." [5]

Like that of their Master such deaths are in reality victories over death. Rarely was there any feverish excitement; the martyrs went to their deaths calmly and joyfully, humbly but proudly, sometimes with a song on their lips. Around the tombs of these elder brothers and sisters in the faith, the young Christian communities renewed their fervor and their confidence as they celebrated their bloodstained anniversaries as *Dies natalis*, their birthday.[6] Over their tombs the Church offered the blood of Christ who had given them the strength to die victoriously.[7]

[3] St. Ignatius of Antioch, *To the Trallians* 2, 1; *To the Magnesians* 3, 1–2.

[4] St. Ignatius of Antioch, *To the Romans* 4, 2 and 5, 3.

[5] St. Ignatius of Antioch, *To the Romans* 6, 3.

[6] *Martyrdom of Polycarp* 18, 3; see Ignatus, *Romans* 6, 1–2.

[7] See the Prayer over the Offerings of Thursday of the III Week of Lent which summarizes the classical teaching of St. Cyprian and others on the relationship between the Eucharist and martyrdom.

Three centuries of irregular but endemic persecution served to make preparation for martyrdom an essential aspect of Christian life, and to make martyrdom itself the official measure of holiness. When the peace of the Church came in the fourth century, Christians had to discover some substitute for martyrdom, and asceticism, virginity, and apostolic charity became such substitutes. Holiness will therefore always be—bloodstained or not—the total gift of oneself to God in Christ.

It should be easy to see that there is no opposition but vital continuity between the exploits of the saints and the mystery of Christ, who "displays, uncovers, and unfolds himself in all his fullness in them." [8] In contemplating and venerating them, it is always Christ whom we celebrate: "You alone are holy, you alone are Lord!" It is Christ manifesting His power and His presence by living victoriously outside the confines of the thirty years of His earthly existence. The liturgy calls him King of apostles, King of martyrs, of confessors, of virgins; all the feasts of the saints are unfailingly Christocentric. The feast of All Saints' concentrates particularly on uniting us to the heavenly liturgy celebrated by the *immense multitude which no man can number* [Apoc. 7, 9], and in an admirable ancient preface, dear to the churches of France, the liturgy proclaims: "In crowning their merits, you crown your own gifts." Finally, to prevent us from resting our hopes on any man, the prayers of the liturgy are addressed to the Father asking Him to do in us what He did in them.

With such perspectives in mind we should have no scruples about looking for example, friendship, and support in the saints. Each one is an example of the "one Model" whom we imitate not by a mechanical and exterior copying, but by living by His spirit and power in an indefinite number of concrete situations. By showing how the Gospel can be lived under all circumstances, the saints teach us how to be both faithful and adaptable, for "there is no more difference between the written Gospel and the lives of the saints than there is between musical notation and music that

[8] J. J. Olier, *Lettre sur la Toussaint,* Ed. Lévesque, number 419, II, p. 418.

is sung." [9] No two voices are alike, and of each saint she canonizes the Church says that there is no one quite like him.[10] Whether it is Irenaeus or John Bosco, Athanasius or the Curé of Ars, Leo the Great or Philip Neri, Thomas Aquinas or Benedict Joseph Labre, Francis Xavier or Theresa of Lisieux, we can always say the same. Each saint is a unique realization of the holiness of Jesus.

If John the Evangelist confessed that the unsearchable riches of Christ could not be set forth in a world of books [Jn. 21, 25], and St. John the Cross felt that "even after all the discoveries of all the holy Doctors of the Church, the greatest portion still remains to be said," [11] we should readily admit that the examples of the saints will make us progress in knowledge of the Lord. *Praecepta docent, trahunt exempla.*[12]

Like the text of the Gospel, the lives of the saints deserve to be lovingly and carefully studied—something that has not always been done in the past. Unfortunately, earlier generations of Christians often let their appetite for the marvelous run away with their historical sense. The declining culture of the antique world and of the early Middle Ages produced many legends and whole series of stereotyped lives unworthy of the name of biographies. Only too often the figure of the man was lost beneath a veneer of edifying but dubious tales.[13]

In the early thirteenth century, Pope Innocent III took steps to protect the Church from questionable canonizations by reserving such solemn declarations to the Holy See. Much later, Urban VIII (1623–1644) completed such procedures, and the new spirit of historical inquiry and passion for accuracy drew some Belgian Jesuits to found an historical society—the Bollandists—whose whole scholarly endeavor was consecrated to restoring and publishing the authentic lives of the saints. The Bollandists and their

[9] St. Francis de Sales, Letter to André Frémiot, October 4, 1604, Ed. d'Annecy XII, p. 306.

[10] Gradual of the first Common of Confessor Bishops.

[11] *Canticle,* strophe 36, 3.

[12] "Men are taught by precepts but drawn by examples."

[13] H. Delehaye is the great authority in the field of hagiography. See his *The Legends of the Saints,* New York, Fordham University Press, 1962.

imitators have demonstrated beyond a doubt that critical accuracy is a necessity and a help to Christian devotion. At times, their contributions were criticized by the devout as too negative, but in the long run even the critics were won over to the cause of authenticity and critical realism. Devotion can hardly be built on anything except truth.

If we want to admire Christ in His saints, we must discover His saving power in them, for "they were not born saints, they became saints."[14] When we celebrate their feasts, we thank and glorify the Lord for their spiritual growth and recognize that their greatness is of God, not of themselves. They were neither Greek heroes nor demi-gods, but brothers and sisters with often the same faults and failings to overcome. Their very limitations and weaknesses make them even more of an example for us so that they become a kind of experimental proof that divine power penetrates the life of this world. "Can't you do what these men and these women did?" asked St. Augustine in his pre-conversion crisis.[15]

When we come to know the saints as they really were, they become almost intimate friends to us. Growing familiarity with their lives and writings makes us look forward to their returning feasts, and ultimately the sanctoral cycle becomes a long list of friends to be welcomed again each year. Because what we admire often expresses the best that is within us, such friendships with the saints bear witness to our authentic desires for holiness. Moreover, fraternal unity in the Body of Christ makes us pray for one another in this world. St. Paul could hardly be thought to have closed off his concern for his fellow laborers now that he enjoys full union with Christ. The same is true for all the saints. Now that they are assured of their own salvation and fully incorporated in the great High Priest, surely they are no less ardent in their prayers than before and no less heard by our heavenly Father. As Bossuet says:

> The Catholic Church teaches us to ask the saints to be our intercessors in the same spirit of fraternal charity and community as we ask the same of our fellow Christians here on

[14] Cardinal Mercier, *La vie intérieure,* 1927, p. 279.
[15] St. Augustine of Hippo, *Confessions* VIII, 27.

earth. The only difference is that the Church believes the prayers of the saints to be far more efficacious by reason of the state of glory in which they now exist.[16]

We must not conclude this introduction to the sanctoral cycle without calling to mind the Queen of Saints. Mary holds a preeminent place in the hierarchy of the saints and in Catholic piety. Yet she is not a mediatory whom Christ interposes between himself and men so that they might keep their distance. On the contrary, she is the means He chose to put an end to all distance so that the human race could, by means of her, touch God directly. God's will for men is wholly accomplished in her. She was entirely at the service of her Son's saving mission, seeming to have no destiny of her own. The only known facts of her life are all events in the life of her Son. Consequently, in the early life of the Church she was never celebrated liturgically save in union with Him. All the early "Marian" feasts of the Roman liturgy were primarily feasts of the Lord, and even later feasts, now classified as Marian, were commemorations of sacred events in Christ's life.

Eastern feasts dedicated to Mary, such as her Nativity and her Falling Asleep, appeared only in the fifth century and were not introduced at Rome until the seventh century. Although few in number originally, they were held in high esteem and celebrated with fervor. Ultimately, Marian feasts multiplied to such an extent that they have come to form a complete cycle closely paralleling that of Christ.

These developments bear witness to the long tradition of intense devotion which Eastern and Western Christians have always felt toward the Mother of God who is also the mother of men.

Because of his boundless love
Jesus
became what we are
that he might make us to be
what he is.

ST. IRENAEUS[17]

[16] Bossuet, Letter to Paul Ferry, July 6, 1666, Ed. Urbain-Lévesque I, p. 155.

[17] St. Irenaeus of Lyons, *Adversus Haereses* V, praefatio; PG 7:1083.

December

Bl. Edmund Campion
St. Francis Xavier
St. Peter Chrysologus
St. Nicholas
St. Ambrose of Milan
The Immaculate Conception
St. Thomas the Apostle

DECEMBER 1
BL. EDMUND CAMPION

Blessed Edmund Campion was one of the new generation of Jesuit missionary priests determined upon the restoration of Protestant England to Catholic unity. Bred in the finest traditions of Oxford University and the Jesuit houses and aflame with zeal for the spiritual authority of the Roman See, Campion returned to England in 1580, labored for a few short months at his spiritual mission, and then crowned what was becoming an impossible task for both him and his companions by steadfast witness under torture and a glorious martyr's death at Tyburn on December 1, 1581.

Halfway through his English career, in answer to the libels and suspicions of the English Government, and to encourage his faint-hearted Catholic brethren, he composed the following defense of his mission and purpose. Nicknamed "Campion's Brag," it became a source of spiritual intoxication for the downhearted and of fury to the persecuting government.

To the Right Honourable Lords of Her Majestie's Privy Council,

Whereas I have come out of Germanie and Boëmeland, being sent by my Superiours, and adventured myself into this noble Realm, my deare Countrie, for the glorie of God and benefit of souls, I thought it like enough that, in this busie, watchful, and suspicious worlde, I should either sooner or later be intercepted and stopped of my course. Wherefore, providing for all events, and uncertaine what may become of me, when God shall haply deliver my body into durance, I supposed it needful to put this writing in a readiness, desiringe your good Lordships to give it your reading, for to know my cause. This doing, I trust I shall ease you of some labour. For that which otherwise you must have sought for by practice of wit, I do now lay into your hands by plaine confession. And to the intent that the whole matter may be conceived in order, and so the better both understood and remembered, I make thereof these ix points or articles, directly, truly and resolutely opening my full enterprise and purpose.

i. I confess that I am (albeit unworthie) a priest of the Catholike Church, and through the great mercie of God vowed now these viii years into the Religion of the Societie of Jhesus. Hereby I have taken upon me a special kind of warfare under the banner of obedience, and eke [also] resigned all my interest or possibilities of wealth, honour, pleasure, and other worldlie felicitie.

ii. At the voice of our General Provost, which is to me a warrant from heaven, and Oracle of Christ, I tooke my voyage from Prage to Rome (where our said General Father is always resident) and from Rome to England, as I might and would have done joyously into any part of Christendome or Heathenesse, had I been thereto assigned.

iii. My charge is, of free cost to preach the Gospel, to minister the Sacraments, to instruct the simple, to reforme sinners, to confute errors—in brief, to crie alarme spiritual against foul vice and proud ignorance, wherewith many my dear Countrymen are abused.

iv. I never had mind, and am strictly forbidden by our Father that sent me, to deal in any respect with matter of State or Policy of this realm, as things which appertain not to my vocation, and from which I do gladly restrain and sequester my thoughts.

v. I do ask, to the glory of God, with all humility, and under your correction, iii sortes of indifferent [impartial] and quiet audiences: the *first* before your Honours, wherein I will discourse of religion, so far as it toucheth the common weale and your nobilities: the *second,* whereof I make more account, before the Doctors and Masters and chosen men of both Universities, wherein I undertake to avow the faith of our Catholike Church by proofs innumerable, Scriptures, Councils, Fathers, History, natural and moral reasons: the *third* before the lawyers, spiritual and temporal, wherein I will justify the said faith by the common wisdom of the laws standing yet in force and practice.

vi. I would be loth to speak anything that might sound of any insolent brag or challenge, especially being now as a dead man to this world and willing to put my head under every man's foot, and to kiss the ground they tread upon. Yet have I such a courage in avouching the Majesty of Jhesus my King, and such affiance [confidence] in his gracious favour, and such assurance in my quarrel, and my evidence so impregnable, and because I know perfectly that no one Protestant, nor all the Protestants living, nor any sect of our adversaries (howsoever they face men down in pulpits, and overrule us in their kingdom of grammarians and unlearned ears) can maintain their doctrine in disputation. I am to sue most humbly and instantly for the combat with all and every of them, and the most principal that may be found: protesting that in this trial the better furnished they come, the better welcome they shall be.

vii. And because it hath pleased God to enrich the Queen my Sovereign Ladye [Elizabeth] with notable gifts of nature, learning, and princely education, I do verily trust that—if her Highness would vouchsafe her royal person and good attention to such a conference as, in the ii part of my fifth article I have motioned, or to a few sermons, which in her or your hearing I am to utter, —such manifest and fair light by good method and plain dealing may be cast upon these controversies, that possibly her zeal of truth and love of her people shall incline her noble Grace to disfavour some proceedings hurtful to the Realm, and procure towards us oppressed more equitie.

viii. Moreover I doubt not but you her Highness' Council being of such wisdom and discreet in cases most important, when you shall have heard these questions of religion opened faithfully, which many times by our adversaries are huddled up and confounded, will see upon what substantial grounds our Catholike Faith is builded, how feeble that side is which by sway of the time prevaileth against us, and so at last for your own souls, and for many thousand souls that depend upon your government, will discountenance error when it is bewrayed, and hearken to those who would spend the best blood in their bodies for your salvation. Many innocent hands are lifted up to heaven for you daily by those English students, whose posteritie shall never die, which beyond seas, gathering virtue and sufficient knowledge for the purpose, are determined never to give you over, but either to win you heaven, or to die upon your pikes. And touching our Societie, be it known to you that we have made a league—all the Jesuits in the world, whose succession and multitude must overreach all the practices of England—cheerfully to carry the cross you shall lay upon us, and never to despair your recovery, while we have a man left to enjoy your Tyburn, or to be racked with your torments, or consumed with your prisons. The expense is reckoned, the enterprise is begun; it is of God, it cannot be withstood. So the faith was planted: so it must be restored.

ix. If these my offers be refused, and my endeavours can take no place, and I, having run thousands of miles to do you good, shall be rewarded with rigour, I have no more to say but to recommend your case and mine to Almightie God, the Searcher of Hearts, who send us His grace, and set us at accord before the day of payment, to the end we may at last be friends in heaven, when all injuries shall be forgotten.

BL. EDMUND CAMPION [101]

THE MARTYRDOM OF FATHER CAMPION

England, look up! Thy soil is stained with blood,
Thou hast made martyrs many of thine own.
If thou hadst Grace, their deaths would do thee good.
The seed will take, which in such blood is sown,
And Campion's learning, fertile so before,
Thus watered too, must needs of force be more.

All Europe wonders at so rare a man.
England is filled with rumour of his end.
London must needs, for it was present then
When constantly three saints their lives did spend.
The streets, the stones, the steps, they hale them by,
Proclaim the cause, for which these martyrs die.

The Tower says, the truth he did defend.
The Bar bears witness of his guiltless mind.
Tyburn doth tell, he made a patient end.
In every gate his martyrdom we find.

In vain you wrought, that would obscure his name,
For heaven and earth will still record the same.

His quartered limbs shall join with joy again,
And rise a body brighter than the sun.
Your bloody malice tortured him in vain,
For every wrench some glory hath him won.
And every drop of blood which he did spend
Hath reaped a joy, which never shall have end.

HENRY WALPOLE [102]

DECEMBER 3
ST. FRANCIS XAVIER

Francis (1506–1552) is for good reasons the patron saint of the missions. While a rather vain and frivolous student at the University of Paris, he became the disciple of Ignatius Loyola—whom he at first despised—made the spiritual exercises under his direction and was won for Christ the King in exemplary fashion. As one of the first members of the Company of Jesus, Xavier was sent by Ignatius to the Orient in order to capitalize on Portuguese contacts with the great heathen world. During his twelve years in the East he became a prodigy of missionary heroism and miracle-working in India, Oceania, and Japan. His letter to Ignatius and to his brother Jesuits in Europe reveal both his fervor and his missionary methods.

To the Society of Jesus at Rome. (1543)

May the grace and charity of Christ our Lord always help and favour us! Amen.

It is now the third year since I left Portugal. I am writing to you for the third time, having as yet received only one letter from you, dated February 1542. God is my witness what joy it caused me. I only received it two months ago—later than is usual for letters to reach India, because the vessel which brought it had passed the winter at Mozambique.

I and Francis Mancias are now living amongst the Christians of Comorin. They are very numerous, and increase largely every day. When I first came I asked them, if they knew anything about our Lord Jesus Christ? but when I came to the points of faith in detail and asked them what they thought of them, and what more they believed now than when they were Infidels, they only replied that they were Christians, but that as they are ignorant of Portuguese, they know nothing of the precepts and mysteries of our holy religion. We could not understand one another, as I spoke Castilian and they Malabar; so I picked out the most intelligent and well read of them, and then sought out with the greatest diligence men who knew both languages. We held meetings for several days, and by our joint efforts and with infinite difficulty we translated the Catechism into the Malabar tongue. This I learnt by heart, and then I began to go through all the villages of the coast, calling around me by the sound of a bell as many as I could, children and men. I assembled them twice a day and taught them the Christian doctrine: and thus, in the space of a month, the children had it well by heart. And all the time I kept telling them to go on teaching in their turn whatever they had learnt to their parents, family, and neighbours.

Every Sunday I collected them all, men and women, boys and girls, in the church. They came with great readiness and with a great desire for instruction. Then, in the hearing of all, I began by calling on the name of the most holy Trinity, Father, Son, and Holy Ghost, and I recited aloud the Lord's Prayer, the Hail Mary, and the Creed in the language of the country: they all followed me in the same words, and delighted in it wonderfully. Then I repeated the Creed by myself, dwelling upon each article singly. Then I asked them as to each article, whether they believed it unhesitatingly; and all, with a loud voice and their hands crossed over their breasts, professed aloud that they truly believed it. I take care to make them repeat the Creed oftener than the other prayers; and I tell them that those who believe all that is contained therein are called Christians. After explaining the Creed I go on to the Commandments, teaching them that the Christian law is contained in those ten precepts, and that every one who observes them all faithfully is a good and true Christian and is certain of eternal salvation, and that, on the other hand, whoever neglects a single one of them is a bad Christian, and will be cast into hell unless he is truly penitent for his sin. Converts and heathen alike are astonished at all this, which shows them the holiness of the Christian law, its perfect consistency with itself, and its agreement with reason. After this I recite our principal prayers, as the Our Father and the Hail Mary, and they say them after me. Then we go back to the Creed, adding the Our Father and the Hail Mary after each article, with a short hymn; for, as soon as I have recited the first article, I sing in their language, "Jesus, Son of the Living God, grant us the grace to believe firmly this first article of your faith: and that we may obtain this from you, we offer you this prayer taught us by yourself." Then we add this second invocation: "Holy Mary, Mother of our Lord Jesus Christ, obtain for us from your most sweet Son that we may believe without hesitation this article of the Christian faith." We do the same after all the other eleven articles.

We teach them the Commandments in the following way. After we have sung the first, which enjoins the love of God, we pray thus: "Jesus Christ, Son of the Living God, grant us the grace to love Thee above all things"; and then we say for this intention the Lord's Prayer. Then we all sing together, "Holy Mary, Mother of Jesus Christ, obtain for us from your Son the grace to observe perfectly the first of His Commandments"; and then we say the Hail Mary. So we go on through the other nine, changing the words of our little invocation as occasion requires. Thus I accustom them to ask for these graces with the ordinary prayers of the Church, and I tell them at the same time that if they obtain them, they will have all other things that they can wish for more abundantly than they would be able to ask for them. I make them all, particularly those who are to be baptized, repeat the form of general confession. These last I question after each article of the Creed as it is recited, whether they believe it firmly; and after they have answered yes, I give them an instruction in their own language explaining the chief heads of the Christian religion, and the duties necessary to salvation. Last of all, I admit them thus prepared to baptism. The instruction is ended by the Salve Regina, begging the aid and help of our Blessed Lady.

As to the numbers who become Christians, you may understand them from this, that it often happens to me to be hardly able to use my hands from the fatigue of baptizing: often in a single day I have baptized whole villages. Sometimes I have lost my voice and strength altogether with repeating again and again the Credo and the other forms.

The fruit that is reaped by the baptism of infants, as well as by the instruction of children and others, is quite incredible. These children, I trust heartily, by the grace of God, will be much better than their fathers. They show an ardent love for the Divine law, and an extraordinary zeal for learning our holy religion and imparting it to others. Their hatred for idolatry is marvellous. . . .

I had been living for nearly four months in a Christian village, occupied in translating the Catechism. A great number of natives came from all parts to entreat me to take the trouble to go to their houses and call on God by the bedsides of their sick relatives. Such numbers also of sick made their own way to us, that I had enough to do to read a Gospel over each of them. At the same time we kept on with our daily work, instructing the children, baptizing converts, translating the Catechism, answering difficulties, and burying the dead. For my part I desired to satisfy all, both the sick who came to me themselves, and those who came to beg on the part of others, lest if I did not, their confidence in, and zeal for, our holy religion should relax, and I thought it wrong not to do what I could in answer to their prayers. But the thing grew to such a pitch that it was impossible for me myself to satisfy all, and at the same time to avoid their quarreling among themselves, every one striving to be the first to get me to his own house; so I hit on a way of serving all at once. As I could not go myself, I sent round children whom I could trust in my place. They went to the sick persons, assembled their families and neighbours, recited the Creed with them, and encouraged the sufferers to conceive a certain and well founded confidence of their restoration. Then after all this, they recited the prayers of the Church. To make my tale short, God was moved by the faith and piety of these children and of the others, and restored a great number of sick persons health both of body and soul. How good He was to them! He made the very disease of their bodies the occasion of calling them to salvation, and drew them to the Christian faith almost by force!

I have also charged these children to teach the rudiments of Christian doctrine to the ignorant in private houses, in the streets, and the crossways. As soon as I see that this has been well started in one village, I go on to another and give the same instructions and the same commission to the children, and so I go through in order the whole number of their villages. When I have done this and am going away, I leave in each place a copy of the Christian doctrine, and tell all those who know how to write to copy it out, and all the others are to learn it by heart and to recite it from memory every day. Every feast day I bid them meet in one place and sing all together the elements of the faith. For this purpose I have appointed in each of the thirty Christian villages men of intelligence and character who are to preside over these meetings, and the Governor, Don Martin Alfonso, who is so full of love for our society and of zeal for religion, has been good enough at our request to allot a yearly revenue of 4000 gold *fanams* for the salary of these catechists. He has an immense friendship for ours, and desires with all his heart that some of them should be sent hither, for which he is always asking in his letters to the King.

ST. FRANCIS XAVIER [103]

end.

DECEMBER 4
ST. PETER CHRYSOLOGUS

Peter, Bishop of Ravenna [*d. 450*], *is famous as one of the greatest early expounders of the word of God. Endowed with extraordinary eloquence, this "golden-tongued" orator has bequeathed to the Church a marvellous series of homilies on the Scripture lessons of the liturgical year.*

On the Lord's Prayer to catechumens.

Dearly beloved, you have received the faith by hearing; now listen to the formula of the Lord's prayer. Christ taught us to pray briefly. He wishes us to put our petitions forward quickly. Why will He not give himself to those who entreat Him, since He gave himself to those who did not ask Him. Or what delay in answering will He show who by formulating prayers has thus anticipated His suppliants' desires?

The angels stand in awe at what you are going to hear today. Heaven marvels, earth trembles, flesh does not bear it, hearing does not grasp it, the mind does not penetrate it, all creation cannot sustain it. I do not dare to utter it, yet I cannot remain silent. May God enable you to hear and me to speak.

What is more awesome: that God gives himself to earth, or that He places you in Heaven? That He himself enters a union with flesh, or that He causes you to enter into a sharing of the Divinity? That He himself accepts death, or that He recovers you from death? That He himself is born into your state of slavery, or that He makes you to be free children of His own? That He takes your poverty upon himself, or that He makes you His heirs, yes, co-heirs of His unique Self?

It is indeed more awesome that earth is transformed into a heaven, that man is changed by a deification, and that those whose lot is slavery get the rights of domination. All this is indeed something to fill us with fear. Nevertheless, the present situation has reference not to the one instructing but to the One who gives the command. Therefore, my little children, let us approach where charity summons, love draws, and affection invites us. May our hearts perceive God as our Father! Our voice should proclaim this, our tongue should utter it, our spirit should shout it aloud; and everything that is in us should be in tune with grace, not fear. For, He who has changed from a judge into a Father has wished to be loved, not feared.

Our Father, who art in heaven. When you say this, do not understand it to mean that He is not on earth, or that He who encompasses all beings is himself contained in a place. But understand that you, whose Father is in heaven, have a lineage derived from heaven. So act, too, that you become your Father's image by your holy way of life. He who does not darken himself with human vices, but shines with virtues like God's, proves himself a son of God.

Hallowed be Thy name. We are called by the name of Him whose offspring we are. Therefore, let us beg that His Name, which is holy in itself and by its very nature, may be treated as holy by us. For, God's Name either gets honored because of our conduct, or blasphemed because of our misdeeds. Hear the Apostle's words: *For the name of God is blasphemed through you among the Gentiles.* [Rom. 2, 24]

Thy kingdom come. Was there ever a time when God did not reign? Therefore we ask that He who always has reigned himself may now reign in us, that we also may be able to reign in Him. The Devil has reigned, sin has reigned, death has reigned, and the human race has long been captive. Consequently, we ask that God may reign in His kingdom, the Devil may be subject, sin may fail, death may die, and the captive human race may be captured in such a way that we may reign as free men unto everlasting life.

Thy will be done on earth as it is in heaven. This is the kingdom of God, when no other will than God's prevails, either in heaven or on earth; when in the case of all men, God is the directing mind, God is living, God is acting, God is reigning, God is everything, so that, according to that statement of the Apostle: *God may be all in all of you.* [1 Cor. 15, 28]

Give us this day our daily bread. He who gave himself to us as a Father, who adopted us as His sons, who made us the heirs of His goods, who raised us up in name and gave us His own honor and kingdom, He has directed that we should ask for our daily bread. In the kingdom of God, in the midst of His divine gifts, why does man in his poverty beg? Is it only when asked that a Father so good, so kindly, so generous gives bread to His children? And what are we to make of His statement: *Do not be anxious about what you are to eat, or what you are to drink, or what you are to put on.* [Mt. 6, 31] Is he telling us to ask for that about which He forbids us to think? What do we hold? The heavenly Father is encouraging us, as heavenly sons, to ask for heavenly bread. He said: *I am the bread that has come down from heaven.* [Jn. 6, 41] He is the Bread sown in the Virgin, leavened in the flesh, molded in His passion, baked in the furnace of the sepulchre, placed in the churches, and set upon the altars, which daily supplies heavenly food to the faithful.

And forgive us our trespasses as we forgive those who trespass against us. O man, if you cannot be without sin, and wish your whole debt to be forgiven you always, you yourself should forgive always. Forgive just as much as you want to be forgiven to yourself. Forgive as often as you want to be forgiven. Indeed, just because you want the whole debt to be forgiven to yourself, you yourself forgive the whole. O man, understand that by forgiving others you have given forgiveness to yourself.

And lead us not into temptation, because in the world life itself is a temptation. *The life of man upon earth is a temptation,* Job says. [7, 1] Therefore let us ask Him not to leave us to our own will, but to hedge us about in our own every act with His fatherly kindness, and by His guidance from heaven to keep us firm on the path of life.

But deliver us from evil. From which evil? Surely, from the Devil, from whom all evil comes. We ask that we be free from evil, because he who has not been free from evil cannot enjoy the good.

ST. PETER CHRYSOLOGUS [104]

DECEMBER 6
ST. NICHOLAS

Although more than half legendary, Nicholas, Bishop of Myra, in Asia Minor, has come down to us as a very great disciple and imitator of Jesus "who went about doing good." The account in the Golden Legend is redolent of this spirit.

Nicholas, citizen of the city of Patras, was born of rich and holy kin, and his father was Epiphanes and his mother Johane. He was begotten in the first flower of their age, and from that time forthon they lived in continence and lead an heavenly life. . . .

He used and haunted gladly holy church; and all that he might understand of holy scripture he executed it in deed and work after his power. And when his father and mother were departed out of this life, he began to think how he might distribute his riches, and not to the praising of the world but to the honour and glory of God. And it was so that one, his neighbour, had then three daughters, virgins, and he was a nobleman: but for the poverty of them together, they were constrained, and in very purpose to abandon them to the sin of lechery, so that by the gain and winning of their infamy they might be sustained. And when the holy man Nicholas knew hereof he had great horror of this villainy, and threw by night secretly into the house of the man a mass of gold wrapped in a cloth. And when the man arose in the morning, he found this mass of gold, and rendered to God therefor great thankings, and therewith he married his oldest daughter. And a little while after this holy servant of God threw in another mass of gold, which the man found, and thanked God, and purposed to wake, for to know him that so had aided him in his poverty. And after a few days Nicholas doubled the mass of gold, and cast it into the house of this man. He awoke by the sound of the gold, and followed Nicholas, which fled from him, and he said to him: Sir, flee not away so that I may see and know thee. Then he ran after him more hastily, and knew that it was Nicholas; and anon he kneeled down, and would have kissed his feet, but the holy man would not, but required him not to tell nor discover this thing as long as he lived. . . .

It was so on a time that all the province of St. Nicholas suffered great famine, in such wise that victual failed. And then this holy man heard say that certain ships laden with wheat were arrived in the haven. And anon he went thither and prayed the mariners that they would succour the perished at least with an hundred muyes of wheat of every ship. And they said: Father we dare not, for it is meted and measured, and we must give reckoning thereof in the garners of the Emperor in Alexandria. And the holy man said to them: Do this that I have said to you, and I promise, in the truth of God, that it shall not be lessed or minished when ye shall come to the garners. And when they had delivered so much out of every ship, they came into Alexandria and delivered the measure that they had received. And then they recounted the miracle to the ministers of the Emperor, and worshipped and praised strongly God and his servant Nicholas. Then this holy man distributed the wheat to every man after that he had need, in such wise that it sufficed for two years, not only for to sell, but also to sow. . . .

And when it pleased Our Lord to have him depart out this world, he prayed our Lord that he would send him his angels; and inclining his head he saw the angels come to him, whereby he knew well that he should depart, and began this holy psalm: *Lord, into thine hands I commend my spirit* [Ps. 30, 6], he rendered up his soul and died, the year of our Lord three hundred and forty-three, with great melody sung of the celestial company. And when he was buried in a tomb of marble, a fountain of oil sprang out from the head unto his feet; and unto this day holy oil issueth out of his body, which is much available to the health of sicknesses of many men. And after him in his see succeeded a man of good and holy life, which by envy was put out of his bishopric. And when he was out of his see the oil ceased to run, and when he was restored again thereto, the oil ran again.

Long after this the Turks destroyed the city of Mirea, and then came thither forty-seven knights of Bari, and four monks showed to them the sepulchre of St. Nicholas. And they opened it and found the bones swimming in the oil, and they bare them away honourably into the city of Bari, [Italy] in the year of our Lord ten hundred and eighty-seven.

THE GOLDEN LEGEND [105]

Let us come together, O feast-lovers, and praise in paeans the comeliness of Bishops, the pride of the fathers, and the fountain of miracles, the great helper of believers, saying, Rejoice, O watchman of the people of Myra, their revered leader and unshakeable pillar. Rejoice, O effulgent star, lighting the utmost corners of the world with miracles. Rejoice, O divine joy of the sorrowful, all-zealous champion of the oppressed. Wherefore, now, O all-beatified Nicholas, you still intercede with Christ God on behalf of those who ever honour faithfully and eagerly your all-festive and joyful memory.

BYZANTINE LITURGY [106]

DECEMBER 7

ST. AMBROSE OF MILAN

Born around 340 of an ancient and renowned Roman family of administrators and politicians, educated in the finest classical tradition of Roman letters, a lawyer and Roman governor in Northern Italy with his headquarters at Milan, Ambrose was quite unexpectedly and against his will elected bishop of that imperial capital while still a catechumen. As bishop, he played a decisive role in the development of the liturgy, transmitted the insights of the great Eastern Fathers to his people by means of his lucid sermons and commentaries on Holy Scripture, composed a remarkable handbook On the Duties of the Clergy *and a series of hymns for the canonical hours which both in Latin and translation stand among the masterpieces of our poetical tradition.*

As bishop of the imperial capital, he set himself to be the voice of conscience for the Roman emperors. As the upholder of the primacy of the spiritual, he threatened Valentinian I with excommunication and imposed public penance on Theodosius the Great. He has often been considered the perfect combination of the virtues of the upright Roman magistrate and the pious Christian.

While still in quest of faith and baptism, Augustine discovered the busy Bishop of Milan to be a man of prayer and study.

I considered Ambrose himself, who was honored by people of such importance, a lucky man by worldly standards; only his celibacy seemed to me rather a burden to bear. But I could neither guess nor tell from my own experience what hope he had within him, what were his struggles against the temptations of his exalted position, what solace he found in adversity; nor could I tell of that hidden mouth of his (the mouth of his heart), what joys it tasted in the rumination of your bread. And he on his side did not know of the turmoil in which I was or the deep pit of danger before my feet. I was not able to ask him the questions I wanted to ask in the way I wanted to ask them, because I was prevented from having an intimate conversation with him by the crowds of people, all of whom had some business with him and to whose infirmities he was a servant. And for the very short periods of time when he was not with them, he was either refreshing his body with necessary food or his mind with reading.

ST. AUGUSTINE [107]

Ambrose the bishop admonishes Theodosius the emperor for the massacre of Thessalonica.

The affair which took place in the city of Thessalonica and with no precedent within memory, that which I could not prevent from taking place, which I had declared would be most atrocious when I entered pleas against it so many times, and which you yourself, by revoking it too late, manifestly considered to have been very serious, this when done I could not extenuate. It was first heard of when the synod had met on the arrival of Gallican bishops. No one failed to lament, no one took it lightly. Your being in fellowship with Ambrose was not an excuse for your deed; blame for what had been done would have been heaped upon me even more had no one said there must needs be a reconciliation with our God.

Are you ashamed, O Emperor, to do what King David the Prophet did, the forefather of the family of Christ according to the flesh? . . . These things I have written not to disconcert you but that the examples of kings may stir you to remove this sin from your kingdom, for you will remove it by humbling your soul before God. You are a man, you have met temptation—conquer it! Sin is not removed except by tears and penance. No angel or archangel can remove it; it is God himself who alone can say: *I am with you* [Mt. 28, 20]; if we have sinned, He does not forgive us unless we do penance.

I urge, I ask, I beg, I warn, for my grief is that you, who were a model of unheard-of piety, who had reached the apex of clemency, who would not allow the guilty to be in peril, are not now mourning that so many guiltless have perished. Although you waged battles most successfully, and were praiseworthy also in other respects, the apex of your deeds was always your piety. The Devil envied you this, your most outstanding possession. Conquer him while you still have the means of doing so. Do not add another sin to your sin nor follow a course of action which has injured many followers.

I among all other men, a debtor to your piety, to whom I cannot be ungrateful, this piety which I discover in many emperors and match in only one, I, I say, have no charge of arrogance against you, but I do have one of fear. I dare not offer the Holy Sacrifice if you intend to be present. Can that which is not allowable, after the blood of one man is shed, be allowable when many persons' blood was shed? I think not.

Lastly, I am writing with my own hand what you alone may read. Thus, may the Lord free me from all anxieties, for I have learned very definitely what I may not do, not from man nor through man. In my anxiety, on the very night that I was preparing to set forth you appeared in my dreams to have come to the church and I was not allowed to offer the Holy Sacrifice. I say nothing of the other things I could have avoided, but bore for love of you, as I believe. May the Lord make all things pass tranquilly. Our God admonishes us in many ways, by heavenly signs, by the warning of the Prophets, and He wills that we understand even by the visions of sinners. So we will ask Him to remove these disturbances, to preserve peace for you who are rulers, that the faith and peace of the Church continue, for it avails much if her emperors be pious Christians.

ST. AMBROSE [108]

Ambrose introduces hymns to the Milanese Church "which [he later said] echoes with refluent waves of the people's prayer, with the responses of psalms, the singing of men, of women, of children, a crashing surf of concordant song."

In those days I could never have enough of the wonderful sweetness of meditating upon the depth of your counsel for the salvation of the human race. What tears I shed in your hymns and canticles! How deeply was I moved by the voices of your sweet singing Church! Those voices flowed into my ears and the truth was distilled into my heart, which overflowed with my passionate devotion. Tears ran from my eyes and happy I was in those tears.

The Church of Milan had only recently begun to practice this kind of consolation and exhortation, and there was great enthusiasm among the brethren as they joined together both with heart and voice in the singing. In fact it was only a year or not much more than a year previously when Justina, the mother of the boy emperor Valentinian, was persecuting your servant Ambrose in the interests of her own heresy (she had been led astray by the Arians). Then the devout congregation stayed day and night in the church, ready to die with their bishop, your servant. In all this anxious watching, my mother, your handmaiden, took a leading part and lived in prayer. I myself had not yet been warmed by the heat of your Spirit, but I was nevertheless stirred up by the state of alarm and excitement in the city. It was then that the practice began of singing hymns and psalms in the manner of the Eastern Churches, so that the people should not grow faint and tired in this time of their sorrow. The custom has been kept from that day to this and has been imitated by many, indeed by almost all, of your congregations in other parts of the world.

ST. AUGUSTINE [109]

Ambrose himself composed some of the finest hymns to enter the Divine Office. The following example was written for use at cock-crow, that is, around daybreak, and has been sung at Morning Praise (Lauds) for centuries.

AT COCK-CROWING

Dread framer of the earth and sky!
Who dost the circling seasons give!
And all the cheerful change supply
Of alternating morn and eve!

Loud crows the herald of the dawn,
Awake amid the gloom of night,
And guides the lonely traveller on,
With call prophetic of the light.

Forthwith at this, the darkness chill
Retreats before the star of morn;
And from their busy schemes of ill,
The vagrant crews of night return.

Fresh hope, at this, the sailor cheers;
The waves their stormy strife allay;

The Church's Rock, at this, in tears,
Hastens to wash his guilt away.

Arise ye, then, with one accord!
Nor longer wrapt in slumber lie;
The cock rebukes all who their Lord
By sloth neglect, by sin deny.

At his clear cry joy springs afresh;
Health courses through the sick man's veins;
The dagger glides into its sheath;
The fallen soul her faith regains.

Jesu! look on us when we fall;
One momentary glance of thine
Can from her guilt the soul recall
To tears of penitence divine.

Awake us from false sleep profound,
And through our senses pour thy light;
Be thy blest name the first we sound
At early morn, the last at night.

ST. AMBROSE [110]

DECEMBER 8
THE IMMACULATE CONCEPTION

The Christian East celebrated a feast of Anne's conception of Mary at an early period. It passed to the West in the seventh century, then disappeared for a time, only to reappear in England in the twelfth century. A Franciscan theologian, John Duns Scotus (1265–1308) was the first to elaborate a theology of the Immaculate Conception, and despite considerable opposition the feast spread rather widely in the fourteenth century. In 1438, the Council of Basel ordered its celebration, and on December 8, 1854, Pope Pius IX, in his encyclical letter Ineffabilis Deus, *defined that "the doctrine which holds the most blessed Virgin Mary was, by the singular favor and privilege of Almighty God in view of the merits of Jesus Christ, the Savior of the human race, preserved free from all stain of original sin from the first instant of her conception, is a doctrine revealed by God and therefore to be firmly and constantly believed by all the faithful."*

Mary the Dawn, Christ the perfect Day.

As soon as the Incarnation is in question, from the very decree that decided it, she is likewise in question. For God as for us, the God-man is man through His mother; and in willing and predestinating Him as man, God also willed and predestined her. God wills the God-man as a fullness of divinization and holiness. But this was to be a divinization and holiness coming to a sinful race and displaying all the greater excellence by the immense restoration to be accomplished.

The same is true of Mary. She is willed as the mother of this fullness and as a condition and an aspect of this outpouring of divinization. Accordingly, she is willed in an order of absolute sanctity, and so, like all that is holy, she is meant to be immaculate. But she is also willed as joined by God to a sinful race, and hence as being in that race and associated with it, and therefore in solidarity with sin. What does this mean if not that the immense restoration willed in Christ was to be realized in her with unequalled fullness, that she was to stem from the sinful race although exempt from sin, and that she was to be wholly immaculate, though by way of preservation and exception? Thus she was willed with the will that willed the Son himself and predestined Him as incarnate, and she was at the same time willed with the will that willed sinful humanity as the matter in which the Incarnation was to be effected. She was to be redeemed as befits one who is, in a certain real sense, the principle of redemption. "As the mother of the Redeemer, she is redeemed in a more sublime way."

This is passive redemption in its perfection, because it is a perfect union with active redemption. At this point of decisive entrance, the Redeemer ought to produce a first, triumphant, absolute effect; otherwise we should have to say that, in a certain sense, He is unequal to His task. This is passive redemption at its origin, in its first and primordial realization; if it has any imperfection at that stage, it will be marred by imperfection throughout its course, and will not be worthy of God. If the redemption was decreed from the beginning, it had to assert its absolute primacy over evil from the outset; it had to be complete.

Therefore no greater purity than Mary's is possible, and Jesus himself is no more exempt from sin than is she who is wholly exempt from sin. The difference between Him and her lies in the reason for the innocence, not in the innocence itself. He is without sin because He is who He is; she is without sin because she is His mother. If she is entirely sinless, the reason is that Christ's holiness shines forth in her and that His holiness is holiness itself. She is the mirror without stain and the image of His goodness.

Dogma is obstinately uncompromising in this matter. One would be a heretic were one to assert that she was sanctified later, or even at the second instant of her existence. The Church insists that there was not the slightest taint of sin in her for a single instant; an object touching the sun cannot be in twilight. In this purity we ought to be able to catch a glimpse of the pure divinity of Him whom it proclaims. For her, therefore, nothing is too pure.

In the same way the dawn has one glorious moment: the moment immediately preceding sunrise. Up to that time, only tentative glimmerings are discernible. First a faint pallor shows in the east, scarcely perceptible in the night. Then the light increases, slowly in the beginning, but later more and more rapidly. An instant comes when the radiance is so triumphant, the light so brilliant, and the brightness so dazzling for eyes accustomed to the dark that the beholder may imagine he is facing the sun itself. Yet it is not the sun, which, however, makes its appearance directly afterward, bursting forth like a ball of fire on the rim of the horizon. Only then do we see what the sun is. Before this moment, deception was possible, so mighty did the sun appear in its herald, the dawn.

Thus it is with the Immaculate Conception. During all the preceding centuries the twilight of Christ was seen from afar, from the first beginnings of His purity and holiness, splendid even then in their effects on our race, although still most obscure in comparison with Him. But the Immaculate Conception is high dawn and the break of day.

EMILE MERSCH [111]

The Immaculate Conception means that Mary possessed grace from the beginning. What does it signify, though, to say that someone has sanctifying grace? This dry technical term of theology makes it sound as though some *thing* were meant. Yet ultimately sanctifying grace and its possession do not signify any *thing,* not even merely some sublime, mysterious condition of our souls, lying beyond the world of our personal experience and only believed in a remote, theoretical way. Sanctifying grace, fundamentally, means God himself, his communications to created spirits, the gift which is God himself. Grace is light, love, receptive access of a human being's life as a spiritual person to the infinite expanses of the Godhead. Grace means freedom, strength, a pledge of eternal life, the predominant influence of the Holy Spirit in the depths of the soul, adoptive sonship and an eternal inheritance.

Mary does not differ from us because she possessed these gifts. It is her possession of them from the beginning, and incomparably, that is the sole difference between her and us. As for the content of this gift, its nature and intrinsic meaning, the eternal Father could not intend anything for the mother of his incarnate Son, without intending it for us too, and giving it to us in the sacrament of justification. For us too he eternally intended this saving grace from the beginning, in his eternity, even though it was only effected in us after the beginning of our earthly, temporal life, in order that it might be plain that it is all his grace, that nothing in our salvation belongs to us of ourselves. God has eternally kept his eternal love in readiness for us too, so that in the moment that we call our baptism, he may come into the depths of our heart. For we too are redeemed, saved, marked with God's indelible seal. We too have been made the holy temple of God. In us too the triune God dwells. We too are anointed, hallowed, filled with the light and life of God. We too have been sent by him, from this beginning, into our life, that we too may carry the light of faith and the flame of love through this world's darkness, to the place where we belong, in his eternal radiance, his eternity.

Are we so different, then, from her who was conceived immaculate? May we not say that God did not will this difference between us principally because he loved us less, and therefore did not give us the gift of grace, which is himself, from the beginning, but rather so that through this difference, the full range of significance of grace might find clear expression? In Mary and her Immaculate Conception it is manifest that eternal mercy from the beginning has enveloped man, and therefore us, children of Adam and Eve, sinners, and so it is clear that God does not leave us unaided. We who first came into existence graceless in soul, proclaim the truth that we are not the beloved children of God by our own powers, not by our intrinsic, inalienable nature, wide and noble though its capacity may be, but only by the sheer grace of God alone, which is given to us, the sinners, without any claim or any merits.

KARL RAHNER [112]

THE HYMN, O GLORIOSA DOMINA

Hail, most high, most humble one!
Above the world, below thy Son;
Whose blush the moon beauteously mars,
And stains the timorous light of stars.
He that made all things had not done
Till He had made Himself thy Son.
The whole World's host would be thy guest,
And board Himself at thy rich breast.
O boundless hospitality!
The Feast of all things feeds on thee.
The first Eve, mother of our Fall,
Ere she bore any one, slew all.
Of her unkind gift might we have
Th' inheritance of a hasty grave:
Quick buried in the wanton tomb
Of one forbidden bit,
Had not a better fruit forbidden it.

Had not thy healthful womb
The World's new eastern window been,
And given us heaven again in giving Him.
Thine was the rosy dawn, that spring the day
Which renders all the stars she stole away.
Let then the agèd World be wise, and all
Prove nobly here unnatural:
'Tis gratitude to forget that other,
And call the maiden Eve their mother.
Ye redeem'd nations far and near,
Applaud your happy selves in her;
(All you to whom this love belongs)
And keep't alive with lasting songs.
Let hearts and lips speak loud and say,
Hail, door of life, and source of Day!
The door was shut, the fountain seal'd,
Yet Light was seen and Life reveal'd.
[The door was shut, yet let in day],
The fountain seal'd, yet life found way.
Glory to thee, great virgin's Son!
In bosom of Thy Father's Bliss.
The same to Thee, sweet Spirit! be done;
As ever shall be, was, and is. Amen.

RICHARD CRASHAW [113]

DECEMBER 21
ST. THOMAS THE APOSTLE

If I do not see the marks of the nails in his hands . . . , I shall not believe. (Gospel)

Mary Magdalen who believed so quickly did less for me than Thomas who doubted for a time. By reason of his doubt he came to touch the scars of His wounds and so removed the wound of doubt from our heart.

ST. GREGORY THE GREAT [114]

Be not unbelieving but believing. (Gospel)

You said: *Unless I touch Him, unless I put my finger in, I shall not believe.* Come touch Me. *Put in your finger and be not unbelieving but believing.* [Jn. 20, 26] I knew your wounds. I have kept My wounds for you. Moreover, putting in his hand certainly confirmed the faith of that disciple. For what is the fullness of faith? That Christ be believed to be not merely Man, that Christ be believed to be not only God, but that He be believed to be both Man and God—that is the fullness of faith because *the Word was made flesh, and dwelt among us.* [Jn. 1, 14]

Therefore, when the wounds and limbs of His Saviour had been presented to him to be touched, the disciple touched them and exclaimed: *My Lord and My God!* [Jn. 20, 28] He touched a Man; he recognized God. He touched flesh; he looked upon the Word, because *the Word was made flesh and dwelt among us.* This Word suffered His flesh to be hung upon a tree; this Word suffered His flesh to be pierced with a lance; this Word suffered His flesh to be placed in a tomb; this Word raised His flesh to life, presented it to the gaze of His disciples, offered it to be touched by their hands. They touch and they cry out: *My Lord and my God! This is the Day which the Lord has made!* [Ps. 117, 24]

ST. AUGUSTINE [115]

Our Lord praised easiness of belief, and condemned hardness of belief. To be easy in believing is nothing more or less than to have been ready to inquire; to be hard of belief is nothing else but to have been loth and reluctant to inquire. Those whose faith He praised had no stronger evidence than those whose unbelief He condemned; but they had used their eyes, used their reason, exerted their minds, and persevered in inquiry till they found; while the others, whose unbelief He condemned, had heard indeed, but had let the divine seed lie by the roadside, or in the rocky soil, or among the thorns which choked it. And here I am led to say, what seems to me, as far as it is reverent to conjecture it, the fault of the holy Apostle St. Thomas. He said that he would not believe that our Lord had risen, unless he actually saw Him. What! is there not more than one way of arriving at faith in Christ? are there not a hundred proofs, distinct from each other, and all good ones? Was there no way of being sure He came from God, except that of seeing the great miracle of the resurrection? Surely there were many others; but St. Thomas prescribed the only mode in which he would consent to believe in Him. This was the case of his countrymen also, for in this point he only did what they had done. The Jews had long been the people of God, and they had the writings of the Prophets. The fulfillment of the prophecies in the Person of our Lord was the most obvious and natural evidence to the Jews that He was the Messias; but they would not accept this evidence, and determined to have another. They determined to be convinced in one particular way, viz., by miracles; and when, out of the superabundant mercy of God, miracles were wrought before their eyes, then they would choose the special kind of miracle which was to convince them, and would not believe, unless it was a miracle to their liking. And hence it was that our Lord said, as I have already quoted His words: *Unless ye see signs and wonders, ye believe not.* [Jn. 4, 48] Hence too He said, on other occasions: *O foolish and slow of heart to believe in all things which the Prophets have spoken.* [Lk. 24, 25] And: *If they hear not Moses and the Prophets, neither will they believe if one rise again from the dead.* [Lk. 16, 31] And: *An evil and adulterous generation seeketh a sign, and a sign shall not be given it, but the sign of Jonas the Prophet.* [Mt. 12, 39] And hence the Jews of Thessalonica are censured, and the Bereans, on the contrary, praised, *who received the word with all eagerness, daily searching the Scriptures, whether these things were so.* It is added, *and many of them believed.* [Acts 17, 11–12] And therefore, in the instance of St. Thomas, I say that, when he was so slow to believe, his fault lay in thinking he had a right to be fastidious, and to pick and choose by what arguments he would be convinced, instead of asking himself whether he had not enough to convince him already; just as if, forsooth, it were a great matter to his Lord that he should believe, and no matter at all to himself. And therefore it was, that, while Christ so graciously granted him the kind of proof he desired, He said to him for our sakes: *Because thou hath seen Me, Thomas, thou hast believed: blessed are they that have not seen, and have believed.* [Jn. 20, 29]

JOHN HENRY NEWMAN [116]

January

St. Antony the Hermit
Church Unity Octave
St. Agnes
The Conversion of St. Paul
St. Polycarp
St. John Chrysostom
St. Francis de Sales
St. John Bosco

JANUARY 17
ST. ANTONY THE HERMIT

The life of St. Antony (251–356) was written by his friend St. Athanasius, Patriarch of Alexandria.

St. Antony lived as a hermit in the deserts bordering on the Nile Valley. As his life wore on, he withdrew further and further into the solitude of the desert in order to avoid the throngs of curiosity seekers who came to him. Despite his desire to be alone with the Alone, he ventured into the great Alexandrian metropolis to encourage the faithful to persevere during the anti-Christian persecutions, and, at a later date, at the invitation of St. Athanasius, to help in the fight against Arianism.

After his conversion temptations came to plague him.

The Devil, the hater and envier of good, could not bear to see such resolution in a young man, but set about employing his customary tactics also against him. First, he tried to make him desert the ascetic life by putting him in mind of his property, the care of his sister, the attachments of kindred, the love of money, the love of fame, the myriad pleasures of eating, and all the other amenities of life. Finally, he represented to him the austerity and all the toil that go with virtue, suggesting that the body is weak and time is long. In short, he raised up in his mind a great dust cloud of arguments, intending to make him abandon his set purpose.

The Enemy saw, however, that he was powerless in the face of Antony's determination and that it was rather he who was being bested because of the man's steadfastness and vanquished by his solid faith and routed by Antony's constant prayer. He then put his trust in the weapons that are *in the navel of his own belly.*

[Job 40, 11] Priding himself in these—for they are his choice snare against the young—he advanced to attack the young man, troubling him so by night and harassing him by day, that even those who saw Antony could perceive the struggle going on between the two. The Enemy would suggest filthy thoughts, but the other would dissipate them by his prayers; he would try to incite him to lust, but Antony, sensing shame, would gird his body with his faith, with his prayers and his fasting. The wretched Devil even dared to masquerade as a woman by night and to impersonate such in every possible way, merely in order to deceive Antony. But he filled his thoughts with Christ and reflected upon the nobility of the soul that comes from Him, and its spirituality, and thus quenched the glowing coal of temptation. And again the Enemy suggested pleasure's seductive charm. But Antony, angered, of course, and grieved, kept his thoughts upon the threat of fire and the pain of the worm. Holding these up as his shield, he came through unscathed.

The entire experience put the Enemy to shame. Indeed, he who had thought he was like to God, was here made a fool of by a stripling of a man. He who in his conceit disdained flesh and blood, was now routed by a man in the flesh. Verily, the Lord worked with this man—He who for our sakes took on flesh and gave to his body victory over the Devil. Thus all who fight in earnest can say: *Not I, but the grace of God with me.* [1 Cor. 15, 10]

ST. ATHANASIUS [117]

Such was the radiance of his example and of his spiritual direction that before Antony died thousands of Christian hermits came to people the Egyptian deserts.

So, then, their solitary cells in the hills were like tents filled with divine choirs—singing Psalms, studying, fasting, praying, rejoicing in the hope of the life to come, and laboring in order to give alms and preserving love and harmony among themselves. And truly it was like seeing a land apart, a land of piety and justice. For there was neither wrongdoer nor sufferer of wrong, nor was there reproof of the tax-collector; but a multitude of ascetics, all with one set purpose—virtue. Thus, if one saw these solitary cells again and the fine disposition of the monks, he could but lift up his voice and say: *How fair are thy dwellings, O Jacob—thy tents, O Israel! Like shady glens and like a garden by a river, and like tents that the Lord hath pitched and cedars beside the waters!* [Num. 24, 5–6]

ST. ATHANASIUS [118]

Before dying Antony addressed his final recommendations to two solitaries who had come to assist him in his old age.

I am going the way of my fathers, as Scripture says, for I see myself called by the Lord. And you—be on your guard and do not bring to naught the asceticism you have practiced for so long. Make it your endeavor to keep up your enthusiasm as though you were but now beginning. You know the demons and their designs, you know how fierce they are, yet how powerless. So, do not fear them; rather, let Christ be your life's breath, and place your confidence in Him. Live as if dying daily, taking heed for yourselves and remembering the counsels you have heard from me. Let there be no communion whatever between you and the schismatics and none at all with the heretical Arians. You know how I myself have kept away from them because of their Christ-attacking false heresy. Show your eagerness to give your allegiance, first to the Lord and then to His saints, *that after your death they may receive you into everlasting dwellings* [Lk. 16, 9] as familiar friends. Give these things your thought, make them your purpose; and if you have any care for me and think of me as a father, do not allow anyone to take my body into Egypt, lest they should keep it in their houses. This was my reason for going to the mountain and coming here. You know how I have always put to shame those who do this and charged them to stop the custom. Therefore, carry out my obsequies yourselves and bury my body in the earth and let what I have said be so respected by you, that no one will know the place but you alone. At the resurrection of the dead I shall receive it back from the Savior incorruptible. Distribute my garments. To Bishop Athanasius give the one sheepskin and the cloak on which I lie, which he gave me but which has worn out in my possession; and to Bishop Serapion give the other sheepskin, and keep the hair shirt for yourselves. And now, my children, God bless you; Antony is going and is with you no more.

ST. ATHANASIUS [119]

JANUARY 18–25
THE WEEK OF UNIVERSAL PRAYER FOR CHRISTIAN UNITY

Although many Christians have always suffered profoundly from the scandal of a divided Christendom, it was not until fairly recently that such sentiments have become organized and directed toward real goals.

In 1895, Pope Leo XIII instituted the Pentecost Novena to hasten "the work of reconciliation with separated brethren." In 1908 two Anglican clergymen, Spencer Jones and Lewis Watson, began a week of prayer for Christian unity between January 18 and January 25, the Conversion of St. Paul. After Watson's conversion to Roman Catholicism, this latter week of prayer was much encouraged by the Catholic hierarchies of various countries and finally by the Holy See itself. Often called the Chair of Unity Octave, it quickly assumed the aspect of a prayer crusade for the conversion of non-Catholics. Like similar movements in various Protestant Churches for the conversion of "the others," it unfortunately has given rise to perhaps more tensions than to reconciliations and can hardly be viewed as fully ecumenical in character.

The magnificent conception of a week of universal prayer "for the unity Christ wills by the means He wills" stems directly from the initiatives taken in 1935 by Father Paul Couturier of Lyons, France. Powerfully encouraged by the dynamic Cardinal Gerlier of Lyons, Father Couturier devoted his life to propagating the Week of Universal Prayer as the foundation stone of modern ecumenism. All who acknowledge Jesus as Lord are invited to unite themselves with the high-priestly prayer of their common Lord "that all may be one." [Jn. 17, 22]

While the liturgy has no proper Mass or Office for these days, it does possess a particularly impressive votive Mass "For the

Unity of the Church" which may be used on the free days of this week of prayer. Composed at the time of the great Western Schism, its Epistle is taken from Ephesians 4 and its Gospel from John 17—Scripture passages of peculiarly ecumenical and irenical importance deserving homiletic and meditative emphasis.

A celebration of this beautiful Mass during the Week of Prayer for Christian Unity is a fine moment to remind people that for the primitive and patristic Church the Eucharistic Banquet was the chief sign and means of Christian fellowship: "We are one body because we all share one bread." [1 Cor. 10, 17] *Certainly, the greatest and most tragic aspect of our separations is that the Eucharist has become a sign of division and of discord, each church excluding from its altar the members of another denomination. And yet all agree upon the sacrament as an effective sign of love and of brotherliness! Surely the many separate Eucharists will conclude in one fellowship meal of loving unity if separated brothers truly seek God's will in repentance and prayer.*

Pope Adrian VI's Instructio to the Diet of Nürnberg, January 3, 1523, after the outbreak of the Lutheran Reformation.

God has permitted this persecution to be inflicted on His Church because of the sins of men, especially of priests and prelates of the Church. We know that for some years now there have been in this Holy See many abominations, abuses of spiritual matters, misuse of authority, and finally all things have become decadent. There is no wonder that sickness has passed from the head to the members, from the pontiffs to the lesser prelates. All of us (that is, prelates), and all ecclesiastics have deviated, each in his own way. For a long time there have been none who have done good, not even one. . . . Wherefore, in what touches on Our office, We promise you that We will use all means, that this Curia first of all, whence perhaps all this evil has issued, shall be so reformed, that just as corruption has passed from here unto all the lesser parts of the Church, so from here the health and reformation of all will proceed. Let no one be astonished, if he should note that not all abuses and errors are immediately corrected by Us. The sickness is indeed inveterate. It is not a simple illness, but a complicated and multiple one. Its cure must proceed step by step, and first we must handle the more grave and dangerous ills lest in our eagerness that everything be reformed at once, we wreck the whole work.

ADRIAN VI [120]

Report of a Select Committee of Cardinals to Pope Paul III on the Reform of the Church, February, 1537.

Most Holy Father, we are quite unable to express how grateful the Christian commonwealth ought to be to the good and great God for setting you in these days over His flock and giving you such a spirit. Indeed, we cannot hope even to understand what gratitude it owes to Him. For the Spirit of God, who, as the prophet says, has shored up the very powers of heaven, had decreed to restore through you the Church of Christ that is now collapsing and indeed almost in ruins, to put a supporting hand to the tottering structure, to raise it to its former nobility and give it back its former beauty. Of this divine intention we are sure—we whom Your Holiness has summoned, whom You have bidden make known to You, without respect for any man or for Your own or anyone else's interest, those abuses, those serious ills, from which the Church of God and especially this Roman Curia has long been suffering. These deadly ills have little by little grown ever more serious and have led to the great shambles that now confront us. Your Holiness knows well the source of these evils: some of the pontiffs who preceded You had *itching ears,* as the Apostle Paul puts it, and *heaped up to themselves teachers according to their lusts* [2 Tim. 4, 3], not to learn from them what their duty was but to find by their skill and cleverness the justification for their own pleasure. The result of this course was to be expected. At all times flattery follows power like a shadow, and truth is always hard-put to reach the ear of princes. But now teachers come forward to proclaim that the Pope is the master of all benefices and, since the master may sell his own property, the pope may not be accused of simony. In like fashion they taught that the pope's wish, whatever its quality, is the norm for his enterprises and actions. The consequence? Whatever he please, he may do. From this source, as from the Trojan horse of old, these many abuses and serious ills have burst forth upon the Church of God. Under them she has struggled, as we see, almost unto despair of her salvation. Report of this situation has reached even to the infidel (please, Your Holiness, believe those who know), and it is the prime reason why he derides the Christian religion. Thus because of us—because of *us!*—the name of Christ is blasphemed among the Gentiles.

CONSILIUM DE EMENDANDA ECCLESIA [121]

Legatine address of Reginald Cardinal Pole at the opening of the Council of Trent, 1546.

Before the tribunal of God's mercy we, the shepherds, should make ourselves responsible for all the evils now burdening the flock of Christ. The sins of all we should take upon ourselves, not in generosity but in justice; because the truth is that of these evils we are in great part the cause, and therefore we should implore the divine mercy through Jesus Christ.

REGINALD POLE [122]

Address of Pope Paul VI at the opening of the second session of Vatican Council II, September 29, 1963.

The council aims at complete and universal ecumenicity—that is at least what it desires, what it prays and prepares for. Today it does so in hope that tomorrow it may see the reality. This council, while calling and counting its own those sheep who belong to the fold of Christ in the fullest and truest sense, opens the door and calls out, too, in anxious expectation to the many sheep of Christ who are not at present within the unique fold.

It is a council, therefore, of invitation, of expectation, of confidence, looking forward towards a more widespread, more fraternal participation in authentic ecumenicity.

We speak now to the representatives of the Christian denominations separated from the Catholic Church, who have nevertheless been invited to take part as observers in this solemn assembly. We greet them from Our heart. We thank them for their participation. We transmit through them Our message—as father and brother—to the venerable Christian communities they represent.

Our voice trembles and Our heart beats the faster both because of the inexpressible consolation and reasonable hope that their presence stirs up within Us, as well as because of the deep sadness We feel at their prolonged separation.

If we are in any way to blame for that separation, we humbly beg God's forgiveness and ask parden too of our brethren who feel themselves to have been injured by us. For our part, we willingly forgive the injuries which the Catholic Church has suffered, and forget the grief endured during the long series of dissensions and separations. May the heavenly Father deign to hear our prayers and grant us true brotherly peace.

We are aware that serious and complicated questions remain to be studied, treated and resolved. We would wish that this could be done immediately on account of the love of Christ that "urges us on." But We also realize that these problems require many conditions before satisfactory solutions can be reached—conditions which are as yet premature. Hence We are not afraid to await patiently the blessed hour of perfect reconciliation.

PAUL VI [123]

Now that the Church is co-extensive with the inhabited globe, the hour has arrived to survey afresh the whole course of Church history. Let each Church in the three great traditions, Roman, Eastern, and Protestant, be studied for the witness it has borne to Christ in the course of its life, whether in the nurture of the saints, in the elucidation or defense of truth, or in its contribution to the effective reign of God among men. Let each be surveyed to discover whatever stains of sin, or marks of shame and error, its history may reveal. Such a study will show that no Church in history can claim a monopoly of insight or sainthood, of evangelical zeal, or transforming power. Those things which God has taught the Church through the glory and shame of the Churches will provide data for an ecumenical theology. A theology of revelation, which cherishes without idolatry the historic Creeds and

Confessions, which studies the life history of the Churches in search of insight regarding Christ and the Church, which embraces within its sweep God's dealing with the new Churches in Asia, Africa, Oceania, and Latin America, can lay the foundation of that theology which is needed by an Ecumenical Church in an ecumenical world.

Let the Churches of the Reformation acknowledge their many sins and shortcomings, admitting freely that the Church can sin and has sinned. In penitence and humility, in faith and in hope, let them prepare themselves for the tasks that await them in the coming time. And about one thing let them be clear. The theological statement to which the Church Universal must look forward in the years ahead must be no doctrinal syncretism or theological dilution. It must have at its heart no pale, lowest denominator formula. Never must the Church sponsor a blanched, eviscerated, spineless statement of Confessional theology. It must give birth in this revolutionary transition time, to a full-blooded, loyally Biblical, unashamedly ecumenical, and strongly vertebrate system of Christian belief.

JOHN A. MACKAY [124]

Unity in love can prepare for unity in faith.

We do not know what is in the divine plan of salvation. But we do know that we ourselves, though we cannot create any final unity in Christendom, must do everything possible to prepare the way for *dynamic* unity, a unity of hearts and minds. If there cannot immediately be unity of faith, let there at least be unity of love. And this love must and will drive us to work in common in public life and to make common cause in our social, cultural, economic and political duties and interests. Nothing but this unity in love can provide the prerequisite foundation for our future unity in faith. It is then not only a moral but also a religious duty. As faith leads to love, so does love to faith.

KARL ADAM [125]

JANUARY 21

ST. AGNES

After the end of the great Roman persecutions of the Church, the virgin-martyrs, heroines of the earlier ages, came to hold pride of place in the minds of the faithful. Agnes (the Pure) united in her person these two glorious attributes of virginity and martyrdom. Much honored in the fourth century, the legends surrounding her name grew with the passage of time until she became depicted more as a type of holiness than as an individual person.

The Lord does not promise to give the same rewards to everyone. Some He says He will number in the kingdom of heaven, others that they shall possess the land, others that they shall see the Father. So too in this case He reveals that the order and holy choir of virgins will be the first to follow in His train as it were into a bridal chamber, into the repose of the new ages. For they were martyrs, not by enduring brief corporal pains for a space of time, but because they had the courage all their lives not to shrink from the truly Olympic contest of chastity. And by resisting the fierce torments of pleasure and fear and grief and other evils that come from men's wickedness, they carry off the first prize before all the rest, being ranked higher in the land of promise.

ST. METHODIUS [126]

Chastely I live for Thee,
And holding my lighted lamps,
My Spouse, I go forth to meet Thee.

ST. METHODIUS [127]

The martyrdom of Agnes.

The grave of Agnes is in the home of Romulus; a brave lass she, and a glorious martyr. Laid within sight of their palaces, this maiden watches over the well-being of Rome's citizens, and she protects strangers too when they pray with pure and faithful heart. A double crown of martyrdom was vouchsafed to her, the keeping of her virginity untouched by any sin, and then the glory of her dying by her own will.

They say it happened that as a young girl in her earliest years, scarce yet marriageable, but warm with the love of Christ, she bravely withstood godless commands, refusing to make herself over to idols and desert her holy faith. For though she was first assailed with many arts, now with seductive words from a smooth-tongued judge, and again with threats of cruel torture, she stood firm with strength indomitable, and even offered her body for the sore torment, not refusing to die. Then said the savage persecutor: "If it is easy for her to overcome the pains and bear the suffering and she scorns life as of little worth, still the purity of her dedicated maidenhood is dear to her. I am resolved to thrust her into a public brothel unless she lays her head on the altar and now asks pardon of Minerva, the virgin whom she, a virgin too, persists in slighting. All the young men will rush in to seek the new slave of their sport." "Nay," says Agnes, "Christ is not so forgetful of his own as to let our precious chastity be lost and abandon us. He stands by the chaste and does not suffer the gift of holy purity to be defiled. You may stain your sword with my blood if you will, but you will not pollute my body with lust." When she had thus spoken he gave order to place the maid publicly at a corner of the square; but while she stood there the crowd avoided her in sorrow, turning their faces away lest any look too rudely on her modesty. One, as it chanced, did aim an impudent gaze at the girl, not fearing to look on her sacred figure with a lustful eye; when behold, a fire came flying like a thunderbolt and with it quivering blaze struck his eyes, and he fell blinded by the gleaming flash and lay convulsed in the dust of the square. His companions lifted him from the ground between life and death and bewailed him with words of lamentation for the departed. But the maiden passed in triumph, singing of God the Father and Christ in holy song because, when an unholy peril fell on her, her virginity won the day, finding the brothel chaste and pure. Some have told that being asked she poured forth prayers to Christ that He would restore sight to the prostrate sinner, and that then the breath of life was renewed in the young man and his vision made perfect.

But this was only the first step that Agnes took towards the court of heaven; then she was granted a second ascent. For frenzy was working up her blood-thirsty enemy's wrath. "I am losing the battle," he complained. "Go draw the sword, soldier, and give effect to our lord the emperor's sovereign commands." When Agnes saw the grim figure standing there with his naked sword her gladness increased and she said: "I rejoice that there comes a man like this, a savage, cruel, wild man-at-arms, rather than a listless, soft, womanish youth bathed in perfume, coming to destroy me with the death of my honour. This lover, this one at last, I confess it, pleases me. I shall meet his eager steps half-way and not put off his hot desires. I shall welcome the whole length of his blade into my bosom, drawing the sword-blow to the depths of my breast; and so as Christ's bride I shall o'erleap all the darkness of the sky and rise higher than the ether. O eternal ruler, open the gates of heaven which formerly were barred against the children of earth, and call, O Christ, a soul that follows Thee, a virgin's soul and a sacrifice to the Father." So saying she bowed her head and humbly worshipped Christ, so that her bending neck should be readier to suffer the impending blow; and the executioner's hand fulfilled her great hope, for at one stroke he cut off her head and swift death forestalled the sense of pain.

PRUDENTIUS [128]

Among us, even maidens climb the steps of virtue mounting to the very sky with their longing for death. What need to mention Thecla, Agnes, and Pelagia, who produced noble offspring, rushing to their death as if to immortality? Amid lions the maidens frolicked and fearlessly gazed on roaring beasts.

ST. AMBROSE [129]

JANUARY 25
THE CONVERSION OF ST. PAUL

Paul pursues Christians, Jesus pursues Paul.

What he had done to the Nazarenes in Jerusalem was no longer enough for him. To track them down, denounce them, have them arrested and beaten with rods, force the weakest to apostasize, and, as he admitted himself, to surpass all the other young Pharisees in violence—all this still seemed insufficient. [Acts 8, 3; 22, 4; 26, 10–11; Gal. 1, 13; 1 Tim. 1, 13] Groups of the new doctrine's followers were forming outside of Palestine, especially in the Jewish communities of Syria; he had determined to bring them into the open and strike them down. . . .

Suddenly a light from heaven shone round him, surpassing the sun in intensity. The traveler fell to the ground, and he heard a voice saying, "Saul, Saul, why dost thou persecute me?" Stammering, he said: "Who art thou, Lord?" And the voice resumed: "I am Jesus, who thou art persecuting." Stunned and trembling, the Pharisee murmured: "Lord, what wilt thou have me do?" And the ineffable voice continued: "Arise and go into the city, and it will be told thee what thou must do; for I have appeared to thee for this purpose, to appoint thee to be a minister and a witness."

A prodigious event, of incalculable importance, without which the whole future of Christianity would have been changed. . . . We may suppose that it impressed the imagination of that age as much as it astounds ours, for the Book of Acts relates it not merely once (in Chapter 9), but on two other occasions (Chapters 22 and 26), and the two latter by the lips of Paul himself. Basically, the three narratives are absolutely identical; the differences bear only on details: whether Paul's companions also fell to the ground, and just what they perceived—a blinding light or a voice uttering incomprehensible words. The authenticity of the fact is indisputable, and the Apostle was to confirm it on several later occasions by decisive allusions in his letters. [1 Cor. 9, 1; 15, 3; Gal. 1, 12, 17] On the road to Damascus, in the midday sun, he found himself face to face with Jesus and heard himself called by name. . . .

Thus was accomplished what we customarily call "the conversion of Saint Paul." If there were in him secret approaches of grace, unknown even to himself, if there were discernible elements which contributed to the staggering psychological shock on the road to Damascus—all this is of secondary importance. The impression which one draws from reading the Book of Acts, and to which Paul himself obstinately attested all his life long, is that while he still believed himself shot through with Judaist convictions he was caught up in an overwhelming event which changed him completely, at a single stroke. His transformation was radical and complete. What he had hated one day he adored the next. And the cause he had fought so violently he was to serve with the same violence. In a single second on the desert trail God had conquered His adversary and bound him to Him forever.

This man whom the Light struck down upon the road was conquered, but in this defeat his heart's most profound desires had been fulfilled. How can we regard him without emotion, and, we must admit, without a sort of envy? Saul . . . Saul of Tarsus . . . more sinful than ourselves, the executioner whose hands were stained with the blood of the faithful, and who had this inconceivable fortune of meeting Christ personally, of being called by name by His voice. Why was it so? Why was this man pointed out? We find ourselves here in the midst of the Pauline mystery of grace where, in the secret designs of Providence, all is obscure, and yet wherein all leads to the one goal, which is the deciding Light. It is towards this goal, towards this Light, that Saul shall henceforth tend. The Christ, Who conquered him, will parade him on the highways of the world, as His captive and His slave. As for Saul, he will find the hours of his life always too few to attest adequately his love for the One who had loved him enough to strike him to the heart.

HENRI DANIEL-ROPS [130]

Personal communion with God finds its expression in the theological activity of faith, hope and love, the essence of life in union with God. Part of the fruitfulness of every sacrament, therefore, is the intensification of such activity in its Christological and ecclesial bearing. Faith in Christ, hope in Christ, love for Christ, with the echoes these call forth in human relations, drawing men together as into a family, with Christ the bond—all this, the true riches of a life lived for God, finds its inward meaning in the sacraments. For here we really experience Christ as the sacrament of our encounter with God, because this theological activity is our only immediate connection with God himself. The God-centred activity of the life of the sacraments is the encounter with Christ as sacrament of the encounter with God, the culminating point of the whole sacramental economy of salvation.

EDWARD SCHILLEBEECKX [131]

JANUARY 26
ST. POLYCARP

This very early Bishop of Smyrna in Asia Minor was the disciple of St. John the Divine and the teacher of St. Irenaeus of Lyons.

The eyewitness account of his martyrdom—the earliest such document outside the New Testament to come down to us—is addressed from "the Church of God which sojourns at Smyrna to the Church of God which sojourns at Philomelium and to all the congregations of the Holy Catholic Church in every place."

Early in the year 156 when Polycarp was some eighty-six years old, the arena at Smyrna resounded with the cries: "Death to those who despise the gods! Arrest Polycarp." Although he hid himself in the outskirts of Smyrna at the insistence of his advisers, he was betrayed by a slave who had been put to the torture.

We are sending you, brethren, a written account of the martyrs and, in particular, of blessed Polycarp, whose witness to the faith as it were sealed the persecution and put an end to it. . . .

As Polycarp entered the arena, a voice was heard from heaven: Be strong, Polycarp, and act manfully. Nobody saw the speaker, but those of our people who were present heard the voice. When he was finally led up to the tribunal, there was a terrific uproar among the people on hearing that Polycarp had been arrested.

So when he had been led up, the proconsul questioned him

whether he was Polycarp, and, when he admitted the fact, tried to persuade him to deny the faith.

He said to him, "Respect your age," and all the rest they were accustomed to say; "swear by the Fortune of Caesar; change your mind; say, 'Away with the atheists!' "

But Polycarp looked with a stern mien at the whole rabble of lawless heathen in the arena; he then groaned and, looking up to heaven, said, with a wave of his hand at them: "Away with the atheists!"

When the proconsul insisted and said: "Take the oath and I will set you free; revile Christ," Polycarp replied: "For six and eighty years I have been serving Him, and He has done no wrong to me; how, then, dare I blaspheme my King who has saved me!"

But he again insisted and said: "Swear by the Fortune of Caesar."

He answered: "If you flatter yourself that I shall swear by the Fortune of Caesar, as you suggest, and if you pretend not to know me, let me frankly tell you: I am a Christian! If you wish to learn the teaching of Christianity, fix a day and let me explain."

"Talk to the crowd," the proconsul next said. "You," replied Polycarp, "I indeed consider entitled to an explanation; for we have been trained to render honor, in so far as it does not harm us, to magistrates and authorities appointed by God; but as to that crowd, I do not think it proper to make an appeal to them."

"Well," said the proconsul, "I have wild beasts, and shall have you thrown before them if you do not change your mind."

"Call for them," he replied; "to us a change from better to worse is impossible; but it is noble to change from what is evil to what is good."

Again he said to him: "If you make little of the beasts, I shall have you consumed by fire unless you change your mind."

"The fire which you threaten," replied Polycarp, "is one that burns for a little while, and after a short time goes out. You evidently do not know the fire of the judgment to come and the eternal punishment, which awaits the wicked. But why do you delay? Go ahead; do what you want."

As he said this and more besides, he was animated with courage and joy, and his countenance was suffused with beauty. . . .

the proconsul, on the other hand, was astounded, and sent his herald to announce three times in the centre of the arena: "Polycarp has confessed to being a Christian." Upon this announcement of the herald, the whole multitude of heathens and of Jews living at Smyrna shouted with uncontrolled anger and at the top of their voices: "This is the teacher of Asia, the father of the Christians, the destroyer of our gods! He teaches many not to sacrifice and not to worship!" Amid this noisy demonstration, they called upon Philip, the minister of public worship in Asia, to let loose a lion upon Polycarp. But he replied he had no authority to do so, since he had already closed the hunting sports. Then they decided with one accord to demand that he should burn Polycarp alive. . . .

The thing was done more quickly than can be told, the crowds being in so great a hurry to gather logs and firewood from the shops and baths! And the Jews, too, as is their custom, were particularly zealous in lending a hand. When the pyre was prepared, he laid aside all his clothes, unfastened the loin cloth, and prepared also to take off his shoes. . . . Without delay the material prepared for the pyre was piled up round him; but when they intended to nail him as well, he said: "Leave me just as I am. He who enables me to endure the fire will also enable me to remain on the pyre unbudging, without the security afforded by your nails."

So they did not nail him, but just fastened him. And there he was, with his hands put behind him, and fastened, like a ram towering above a large flock, ready for sacrifice, a holocaust prepared and acceptable to God! And he looked up to heaven and said:

> O Lord God, O Almighty, Father of Thy beloved and blessed Son Jesus Christ, through whom we have received the knowledge of you—God of angels and hosts and all creation—and of the whole race of saints who live under your eyes! I bless Thee, because Thou hast seen fit to bestow upon me this day and this hour, that I may share, among the number of the martyrs, the cup of Thy Anointed and rise to eternal life both in soul and in body, in virtue of the immortality of the Holy Spirit. May I be accepted among them in

Thy sight today as a rich and pleasing sacrifice, such as Thou, the true God that cannot utter a falsehood, hast prearranged, revealed in advance, and now consummated. And therefore I praise Thee for everything; I bless Thee; I glorify Thee through the eternal and heavenly High Priest Jesus Christ, Thy beloved Son, through whom be glory to Thee together with Him and the Holy Spirit, both now and for the ages yet to come. Amen.

When he had wafted up the *Amen* and finished the prayer, the men attending to the fire lit it; and when a mighty flame shot up, we, who were privileged to see it, saw a wonderful thing; and we have been spared to tell the tale to the rest. The fire produced the likeness of a vaulted chamber, like a ship's sail bellying to the breeze, and surrounded the martyr's body as with a wall; and he was in the centre of it, not as burning flesh, but as bread that is baking, or as gold and silver refined in a furnace! In fact, we even caught an aroma such as the scent of incense or of some other precious spice.

At length, seeing that his body could not be consumed by fire, those impious people ordered an executioner to approach him and run a dagger into him. This done, then issued [a dove and] a great quantity of blood, with the result that the fire was quenched and the whole crowd was struck by the difference between unbelievers and elect. And of the elect the most wonderful Polycarp was certainly one—an apostolic and prophetic teacher in our times, and a bishop of the Catholic Church at Smyrna. . . .

By his patient endurance he overcame the unjust magistrate, and thus won the incorruptible crown; and now, exulting with the Apostles and all the saints, he glorifies God and the Father Almighty, and blesses Our Lord Jesus Christ, the Savior of our souls, the Captain of our bodies, and Shepherd of the world-wide Catholic Church.

THE MARTYRDOM OF ST. POLYCARP [132]

JANUARY 27
ST. JOHN CHRYSOSTOM

Born in 344 and well-educated in the humanist culture of his era, John embraced the ascesis of the desert at an early age. Forced to abandon the desert by poor health, he was ordained a priest of Antioch in 386 and there won the name "Golden Mouth" by reason of his eloquence. Created Patriarch of Constantinople by imperial intervention in 397, he became a courageous preacher and defender of the ideals of Christian moral perfection, and as a result incurred the enmity of many courtiers, and even of the Empress Eudoxia. He was later exiled and cruelly maltreated by his guards, and died of exhaustion and exposure in 407.

He whom even his contemporaries surnamed with the resounding title "John of the Golden Mouth" was a little man of somewhat feeble complexion with a rather handsome but emaciated face, very sensitive by nature, and eaten up with zeal for God from his very youth. Ever since Christianity has appeared on earth, there have sprung up such souls in whom the love of Christ has burned like a living flame; but few have attained to the degree of passionate ardor, at once heroic and tender, to the vehemence of affirming the faith and submitting to the orders of his sole Teacher, as this little Syrian deacon become the outstanding bishop-preacher of the Near East.

HENRI DANIEL-ROPS [133]

Blessings flowing from the fountain of marriage.

From this union of man and wife in love great benefits are produced both to families and to states. There is nothing which so tempers our life together as the love of a man and wife. For this love men will lay aside arms. For this love men will give up their own lives. St. Paul would never without a reason and an object, have taken so much pains with this subject. He writes: *Wives, submit yourselves to your husbands, as to the Lord.* [Eph. 5, 22]

Why? Because when husband and wife are in harmony, the children, too, are well brought up, and the domestic help is in good order, and the neighbors, friends, and relations partake of the fragrance of the love of husband and wife. But if husband and wife do not love each other as Christ loves His Bride, the Church, everything is turned upside down and thrown into confusion. . . .

Now what is fitting behavior for the wife, and what for the husband, St. Paul states accurately, charging the wife to reverence the husband as the head, and the husband to love her as a wife; but how, it may be said, can these things be? That they ought indeed to be so, he has proved; but how can they be so? I will tell you. These things will be so if we will but despise money; if we will look but to one thing: Excellence of Soul; if we will keep the Fear of God before our eyes. For as he says in his discourse to servants: *Whatsoever any man does, whether it be good or evil, the same shall he receive of the Lord.* [Eph. 6, 8] It is therefore not so much for her sake that he should love her, as for Christ's sake. This, at least, he as much as intimates, in saying *as unto the Lord.* . . .

Show her, too, that you set a high value on her company, and that you are more desirous to be at home for her sake than in public places. And esteem her before all your friends and above all the children that are born of her, and let these very children be beloved by you for her sake. If she does any good act, praise and admire it; if any foolish one, and such as girls may chance to do, advise and admonish. Condemn up and down all riches and extravagance, and gently point out the ornament that there is in neatness and in modesty; and be continually teaching her what is expedient.

Let your prayers be in common. Let each go to Church; and let the husband ask his wife at home, and she again ask her husband, the account of the things which were said and read there. If any poverty should overtake you, cite to her the example of those holy men, Peter and Paul, who were more glorious than any kings or rich men; and yet how did they spend their lives?—yes, in hunger and thirst. Teach her that there is nothing in life terrible, save only offending against God.

If any marry thus, if he marry with these views, he will be but little inferior to solitaries, the married will be but little below the unmarried.

If you have a mind to give dinners and to make entertainments, invite no immodest, no disorderly person, but if you should find any poor saint, able to bless your home, able only just by setting his foot in it to bring in the whole blessing of God, invite him.

And I would say moreover another thing: Let no one of you make it his endeavor to marry a rich woman, but much rather a poor one. When she comes in she will not bring so sure a source of pleasure from her riches as she will bring annoyance from her taunts, from her demanding more than she brought, from her insolence, her extravagance, her vexatious language. For she will say perhaps: "I have not yet spent anything of yours, I am still wearing my own apparel, bought with what my parents settled upon me."

And what could be more miserable than this language? Why, when you are no longer two but are become one flesh, are your possessions then twofold and not one? Oh! that love of money! You both are become one person, one living creature; and do you still talk of "my own"? Cursed and unholy word that it is: the devil introduced it. Things far nearer and dearer to us than these has God made all common to us, and are these then not common? We cannot say, "My own light, my own sun, my own water." All our great blessings are common, and are riches not so? Perish the riches ten thousand times over! Or rather not the riches, but those tempers of mind which know not how to make use of riches, but yet esteem them above all things.

Teach her these lessons also with the rest, but with all the attractiveness of which you are capable. For since the recommendation of virtue has in itself much that is stern, and especially to a young and tender girl, whenever discourses on true wisdom are to be made, devise every method to make them attractive. And, above all, banish this notion of "mine and thine" from her soul. If she says the word mine, say to her, "What things do you call yours? For, in truth, I know not; I have nothing of my own. How then do you speak of mine when all things are yours."

Freely grant her the word. Do you not see that such is our practice with children? When, while we are holding anything, a child snatches it and wishes again to get hold of the other thing, we allow it, and say, "Yes, and this is yours, and that is yours." . . .

And again, never call her simply by her name, but with terms of endearment, with honor, with exceeding affection. Honor her, and she will not need honor from others. She will not want the glory that comes from others if she enjoys that which comes from you. Praise her before all, on every account, both for her beauty and her discernment. Thus you will persuade her to give heed to none that are without, but to scorn all the world except yourself. Teach her the fear of God, and all things will flow in smoothly to you as from a fountain, and the house will be full of ten thousand blessings. If we seek the things that are incorruptible, these corruptible things will follow. *For,* says He, *seek first the kingdom of God, and all these things will be added unto you.* [Mt. 6, 33]

ST. JOHN CHRYSOSTOM [134]

JANUARY 29
ST. FRANCIS DE SALES

In the tradition of Thomas More and other devout humanists of an earlier century, Francis de Sales (1567–1622) was the formulator of a new type of spirituality for those living in the world. A gentleman peculiarly sensitive in language and in bearing, a humanist open to all that was courteous, elegant, and beautiful, an incomparable friend at once tender and upright, Francis became a careful and penetrative spiritual director. "To people in the world he proposes the true humanist ideal of inconspicuous but very real piety which was to attract and not repel all who came in contact with it." His brilliant career at the universities of Paris and Padua in conjunction with his devout humanism fitted him to be one of the great apostles of the seventeenth century, prince-bishop of Geneva, and cofounder with St. Jane Frances de Chantal of the Order of the Visitation. "A rare bird, this Bishop of Geneva," said Henri IV who was famous for his apt summing-up of character, "he is devout and also learned; and not only devout and learned but at the same time a gentleman. A very rare combination."

Letter of October 13, 1594, to Madame Marie Bourgeois Brûlart of Dijon, Burgundy, on true devotion.

You ask how you should set about acquiring devotion and peace of mind. A very comprehensive question, my dear sister, but I will try and see what I can do for you, as you have every right to ask me. Now listen carefully please. The virtue of devotion is a general inclination and readiness to do what we know to be pleasing to God; it is that opening out of the heart to God of which David said: *I have run in the way of thy commandments, when you did enlarge my heart.* [Ps. 108, 32] Ordinarily good people walk in God's ways, but the devout run, and the really devout run swiftly. I will give you a few rules to keep if you want to be really devout.

The first thing is to obey God's general commandments which apply to all faithful Christians; failing this, as everyone knows, there can be no sort of devotion. Over and above the general commandments you should carefully observe the particular commandments which concern your state of life; anyone who neglects to do this, even if he were to raise the dead to life, is in a state of sin and will be damned if he dies in this frame of mind. Bishops, for instance, are commanded to visit their flock, to teach, correct and console: if I were to spend the whole week praying and all my life fasting while yet neglecting my duty towards my people, then I should be lost. A married person may work miracles and yet refuse the marriage debt to her partner, or neglect the children; in that case she is being worse than unfaithful, says St. Paul [1 Tim. 5, 8]; and this applies in other similar cases. These two kinds of commandments faithfully observed should then form the basis for all devotion; and yet the virtue of devotion does not consist in merely observing them but in doing so promptly and willingly. Now there are several things to be considered if you want to acquire this promptness in the service of God.

Firstly, it is God's will we are fulfilling, and this is precisely why we should hasten to do it, for we are in this world for no other purpose. Alas! Every day we ask for his will to be done, and when it comes to doing it, we find it so hard! We offer ourselves to God so often, saying over and over again: Lord, I am yours, I give you my heart; and when it actually comes to the point we are so cowardly! How can we go on saying that we belong to him if we are not prepared to make our will fit in with his?

Next we should consider what God's commandments are like: gracious, gentle and sweet. This goes not only for his general commandments but more especially for those connected with our state of life. What is it, then, that makes them hard for you? Nothing, surely, except your own self-will which wants to dominate you at all costs and which rejects the very thing it might well want to do if it were not a matter of commandment. From amongst a great number of delicious kinds of fruit Eve chose the forbidden one, and if she had been free to eat it she would very probably not have wanted it. The fact is, we want to serve God, but according to our own will, not his. Saul was told to destroy everything he found in Amalek: he destroyed all except those things he considered precious enough to be offered as a sacrifice, but God said that he would not have sacrifice against obedience. God commands me to serve souls and I want to give myself up to contemplation: the contemplative life is good, but not if it interferes with obedience. It is not for us to choose according to our own will; we must find out what God wants, and if God intends us to serve him in one thing we must not want to serve him in another. God wants Saul to serve him as a king and a captain, and Saul wants to serve him as a priest. The latter is unquestionably the more perfect office; all the same, God will not have this, he wants to be obeyed.

Another good instance: God gave the children of Israel manna in the desert, a most delicious food; and what happens? They do not want it but set their heart on the garlic and onions of Egypt. Our miserable nature always wants to have things its own way and not God's way. As we come to have less self-will we shall find it easier to obey God's will.

Thirdly, you must consider that every state of life is in some way irksome, bitter and unpleasant; and what is more, except for those who are wholly resigned to God's will, people are all inclined to want to change places with others. Bishops would rather not be bishops, married people would rather be single, and single people would like to get married. How can we account for this general restlessness except by admitting a certain innate rebellion against constraint of any kind, and a certain perverse disposition which makes us feel that everyone else is better off than we are? But it is all no good; whatever we do we shall never find rest unless we are wholly resigned. No place is comfortable to those who are sick of a fever: they spend a quarter of an hour in one bed and then they want to change over to another. There is nothing wrong with the bed but the trouble is that their own fever torments them wherever they find themselves. A person who is not suffering from the fever of his own self-will puts up with everything; provided that he is serving God he does not care in what capacity God uses him, and as long as he is doing God's divine will he has no personal preference.

But that is not all. Not only should we want to do God's will, but do it cheerfully, if we are going to be devout. If I were not a bishop, may be that knowing what I do know, I should not want to be one. But seeing that I am already a bishop, I am not only obliged to do what this hard calling requires of me; ever and above that I must do it joyfully, finding pleasure and happiness in it. This is what St. Paul says: each of you is to remain in the condition in which he was called before God. [1 Cor. 7, 24] We have each got to carry our own cross, not anybody else's; and this means renouncing yourself, that is, your own will, according to Our Lord's desire. I should like this or that, I should do much better in some other place—ideas like that are a temptation. Our Lord knows quite well what he is about; let us do what he wants and stay where he has put us. . . .

ST. FRANCIS DE SALES [135]

Letter of January 1, 1608, to the Baronne de Chantal, on the name of Jesus.

I am so hard pressed that the only thing I have time to write to you is the great word of our salvation: JESUS. O, my daughter, if we could only for once really say this sacred name from our heart! What sweet balm would spread to all the powers of our spirit! How happy we should be, my daughter, to have only Jesus in our understanding, Jesus in our memory, Jesus in our will, Jesus in our imagination! Jesus would be everywhere in us, and we should be all in him. Let us try this, my very dear daughter; let us say this holy name often as best we can. And even if at present we can only say it haltingly, in the end we shall be able to say it as we should. But how are we to say this sacred name well? For you ask me to speak plainly to you. Alas, my daughter, I do not know; all I know is if we are to say it well our tongue must be on fire, that is, we must be saying it moved only by divine love which alone is capable of expressing Jesus in our lives and of imprinting him in the depths of our heart. But courage, my daughter, surely we will love God, for he loves us. Be happy about this and do not let your soul be troubled by anything whatever.

ST. FRANCIS DE SALES [136]

JANUARY 31

ST. JOHN BOSCO

John Bosco (1815–1888) would be a worthy patron of organizers and Catholic actionists. The son of peasants, he had the most extraordinary sense of what was practical, of what kind of works would succeed in extending the kingdom of God. Not only was he the founder of two religious congregations and a multitude of works of mercy, but also a wonderworker and a confessor and spiritual director beyond compare. As an educator, Father Bosco proposed to lead adolescents to Christ by means of love and respect, especially those who were hungry for bread and affection.

Don Bosco's method.

A work founded upon authority has some chance of survival, for authority can be passed on. It descends from the great to the small in hierarchical order, each one using his power to keep the one below him in place. But a work founded upon liberty should, humanly speaking, engender only anarchy. And Don Bosco's was founded upon liberty.

He saw before him the mind of a child. He refused to constrain it. College for him was the very antithesis of a barracks or a prison. It was a place of election, wind-swept, living, where souls and bodies must grow together to their flowering. There must be a minimum of discipline in the classroom, complete liberty outside it. That liberty is not so much watched over by the master as observed, directed and gradually shaped. The master must approach each boy, must take interest in all that interests the boy—his family, his work, his tastes, his pleasures—as much as a friend of his own age could, or even more; he must win his confidence and affection and use them effortlessly to inculcate in the boy a knowledge of good and evil, desire for the best, horror of sin, a taste and need for prayer. Above all, prayer and trust in God and the sense of the presence of God must not be reserved for certain times or certain places. They actually came out of church for their evening prayer, that they might learn to pray everywhere. The young must not be stupefied by sermons. These should be short, familiar, plentifully illustrated, within their grasp. The evening prayer for which the boys gather in the yard should last two or three minutes, not more, an incident in their play, as joyful, as pleasant to them.

Since the master has taken so keen an interest in whatever games the boys are playing, they in turn will naturally take as keen an interest in the sermonette he gives them. In the course of the day he must make this or that incident the occasion of a simple, brief sermon; he will be listened to and listened to with pleasure; because it will be knit into the main background of the day. Establish the child's life on the plane of joy, and hence of love; the love of God will surely follow the love of the master. There must be no going in a body to confession or communion. Those who want to receive the sacraments are free to do so, no one is forced to: it is the master's job to win the unwilling boy to the sacraments.

And if a boy has behaved badly, he must be punished only in the last extremity, and that without humiliation or violence; if possible, the worst of the punishment should be the master's sorrow. Obviously punishment of this sort could only be effective if there were real affection between master and boy; and, equally obviously, in the hands of the wrong kind of master the whole thing could be intolerably sentimental. One can only say that, as it actually works in Salesian schools, it is not so.

If an incurably bad boy is found in the class he must be expelled without scandal, on some pretext that will not damage his reputation. For obviously among this vast number of boys it is not to be supposed that all will yield to affection. Some certainly fail to do so. But at least an effort should be made to win the majority. That was Don Bosco's method.

HENRI GHEON [137]

February

St. Ignatius of Antioch
The Purification
St. Romuald
The Chair of St. Peter
St. Matthias

FEBRUARY 1
ST. IGNATIUS OF ANTIOCH

Ignatius, the third successor of St. Peter as Bishop of Antioch, was carried in chains from Syria to Rome so that he might die in the inaugural games of the Colosseum during the Emperor Trajan's persecution (c. 110 A.D.*). On the way to his martyrdom, he wrote seven letters to several churches in Asia Minor and to the Roman Church. Each is a precious testimony of his love for "Christ our God," to his willingness to die for Christ, and to his zeal for Church unity in the Eucharist and under the authority of bishops.*

To the Ephesians.

It is proper for you to act in agreement with the mind of the bishop; and this you do. Certain it is that your presbytery, which is a credit to its name, is a credit to God; for it harmonizes with the bishop as completely as the strings with a harp. This is why in the symphony of your concord and love the praises of Jesus Christ are sung. But you, the rank and file, should also form a choir, so that, joining the symphony by your concord, and by your unity taking your key note from God, you may with one voice through Jesus Christ sing a song to the Father. Thus He will both listen to you and by reason of your good life recognize in you the melodies of His Son. It profits you, therefore, to continue in your flawless unity, that you may at all times have a share in God. . . .

ST. IGNATIUS OF ANTIOCH [138]

To the Magnesians.

At your meetings there must be one prayer, one supplication, one mind, one hope in love, in joy that is flawless, that is Jesus Christ, who stands supreme. Come together, all of you, as to one temple and one altar, to one Jesus Christ—to Him who came forth from one Father and yet remained with, and returned to, one.

ST. IGNATIUS OF ANTIOCH [139]

To the Romans.

I am writing to all the Churches and state emphatically to all that I die willingly for God, provided you do not interfere. I beg you, do not show me unseasonable kindness. Suffer me to be the food of wild beasts, which are the means of my making my way to God. God's wheat I am, and by the teeth of wild beasts I am to be ground that I may prove Christ's pure bread. Better still, coax the wild beasts to become my tomb and to leave no part of my person behind: once I have fallen asleep, I do not wish to be a burden to anyone. Then only shall I be a genuine disciple of Jesus Christ when the world will not see even my body. Petition Christ in my behalf that through these instruments I may prove God's sacrifice. Not like Peter and Paul do I issue any orders to you. They were Apostles, I am a convict; they were free, I am until this moment a slave. But once I have suffered, I shall become a freedman of Jesus Christ, and, united with Him, I shall rise a free man. Just now I learn, being in chains, to desire nothing.

All the way from Syria to Rome I am fighting wild beasts, on land and sea, by day and night, chained as I am to ten leopards, that is, a detachment of soldiers, who prove themselves the more malevolent for kindnesses shown them. Yet in the school of this abuse I am more and more trained in discipleship, although I am not therefore justified. [1 Cor. 4, 4] Oh, may the beasts prepared for me be my joy! And I pray that they may be found to be ready for me. I will even coax them to make short work of me, not as has happened to some whom they were too timid to touch. And should they be unwilling to attack me who am willing, I will myself compel them. Pardon me—I know very well where my advantage lies. At last I am well on the way to being a disciple. May nothing seen or unseen [Col. 1, 16] fascinate me, so that I may happily make my way to Jesus Christ! Fire, cross, struggles with wild beasts, wrenching of bones, mangling of limbs, crunching of the whole body, cruel tortures inflicted by the devil—let them come upon me, provided only I make my way to Jesus Christ.

Of no use to me will be the farthest reaches of the universe or the kingdoms of this world. I would rather die [1 Cor. 9, 15] and come to Jesus Christ than be king over the entire earth. Him I seek who died for us; Him I love who rose again because of us. The birth pangs are upon me. Forgive me, brethren; do not obstruct my coming to life—do not wish me to die; do not make a gift to the world of one who wants to be God's. Beware of seducing me with matter; suffer me to receive pure light. Once arrived there, I shall be a man. Permit me to be an imitator of my suffering God. If anyone holds Him in his heart, let him understand what I am aspiring to do; and then let him sympathize with me, knowing in what distress I am.

The Prince of this world is resolved to abduct me, and to corrupt my Godward aspirations. Let none of you, therefore, who will then be present, assist him. Rather, side with me, that is, with God. Do not have Jesus Christ on your lips, and the world in your hearts. Give envy no place among you. And should I upon my arrival plead for your intervention, do not listen to me. Rather, give heed to what I write to you. I am writing while still alive, but my yearning is for death. My Love has been crucified, and I am not on fire with the love of earthly things. But there is in me a *Living Water* [Jn. 4, 10; 7, 38], which is eloquent and within me says: "Come to the Father." I have no taste for corruptible food or for the delights of this life. *Bread of God* [Jn. 6, 33] is what I desire; that is, the Flesh of Jesus Christ, who was of the seed of David [Jn. 7, 42; Rom. 1, 3]; and for my drink I desire His Blood, that is, incorruptible love.

ST. IGNATIUS OF ANTIOCH [140]

FEBRUARY 2
THE PURIFICATION OF THE BLESSED VIRGIN MARY

Today's feast, according to a new rubric in the Roman Missal, *is actually "a feast of Our Lord." Moreover, the feast commemorates primarily neither the Purification of Mary nor the presentation of Jesus in the Temple, but rather Our Lord's meeting with Simeon. The secondary theme of the day's liturgy, that of "Christ the Light of the World," is inspired by Simeon's reference to him as a "light of revelation to the Gentiles."* [*Lk. 2, 32*]

Today's liturgical ceremony recalls a meeting which took place nearly two thousand years ago. But the purpose of the commemoration is to provide a setting for another meeting which actually takes place today. And this second meeting is in reality a preparation for yet a third meeting destined to take place in the uncertain future. Thus we have here the three layers of the history of salvation which we find in all liturgical commemorations: a past event commemorated and realized in the present with a view to the future.

The meeting of Simeon with Christ in the temple of Jerusalem is being recalled. But this is a figure of *our* meeting with Christ at Mass and holy Communion in the church today. This in turn is a preparation for, as well as a pledge and figure of our meeting with him forever in the heavenly Jerusalem. . . .

Simon, who *came by the Spirit into the temple* [Lk. 2, 27], was in the line of true prophets, and he reaffirmed the plan of God for the salvation of all mankind. He confirmed that Christ was the fulfillment of the prophecies, a light of revelation to the whole world.

At Mass today we hold lighted candles in our hands during the Gospel and again during the sacrificial part of the Mass. Our action is an expression of our belief that Christ is really present to us today in the mystery we celebrate: as our light, enlightening our minds in the Gospel; and as our salvation, giving life to our souls in the Sacrifice of the Mass.

JOHN O'DONNELL [141]

Mary is purified, although she is the noblest flower and the purest glory of Israel. She humbly submits to the law of the Temple, empty as it is of the ark of witness, whilst she herself is the temple of the Holy Spirit, the ark of the new covenant. Jesus is redeemed according to the law of Moses, yet he is himself the redeemer, the *go'êl,* not only of Israel, but of the whole world. He is presented in the Temple, but he is greater than the Temple [Matt. 12, 6]; it is he who sanctifies the Temple and every offering men can make to God.

Jesus is welcomed in the Temple by two representatives of the Poor of the House of Israel who were awaiting the Comforter of their nation: Simeon and Anna the prophetess, two old people, for the former Dispensation has grown old and is nearing the end of its life. Simeon too is a prophet. In a mysterious way he sees Jesus as destined to be "a sign which men will refuse to recognize." Thus he foresees from afar the paschal drama which will replace the old Temple by the new. The whole of Israel's expectation is summed up in the persons of Simeon and Anna. In them Israel through Simeon's prophecy accepts the fact that she must give place to reality and be superseded by it:

> *Ruler of all, now dost thou let thy servant go in peace, according to thy word; for my own eyes have seen that saving power of thine which thou hast prepared in the sight of all nations. This is the light which shall give revelation to the Gentiles, this is the glory of thy people Israel.* [Lk. 2, 29–32]

The prophetic theme of this first "coming" of Jesus to the Temple is already the same as that of the second, when he comes to purify the Temple. The first feature in the new reality Christ brings is the universal scope of salvation; God's house will be open to all nations. This universal significance of the Presentation completes the earlier meaning of the hidden coming of Christmas Day, when the angels and men of every condition acclaimed or acknowledged the Lord. The advent of Jesus and his first coming to the Temple thus take on a cosmic character. They both incorporate and answer the Temple's own cosmic prayer since they foreshadow the time when the whole creation will once more become the temple of God.

YVES CONGAR [142]

FEBRUARY 7
ST. ROMUALD

Hermit, abbot, founder of the Camaldolese Congregation which combines in a remarkable way the hermit and the common life, Romuald (950–1027) was the very model of the contemplative existence intent upon God alone.

O blessed solitude! O sole beatitude!

Now I would like to say a little about the merits of the solitary life and to give you some idea of what I feel about the heights of that life by my praises rather than by my arguments. The solitary life is indeed a school of heavenly learning, a training in divine arts. There all that we learn is God; He is the way by which we proceed and through which we come to a knowledge of the highest truth. The hermitage is a paradise of delight where the fragrant scents of the virtues are breathed forth like sweet sap or glowing spice-flowers. There the roses of charity blaze in crimson flame and the lilies of purity shine in snowy beauty, and with them the humble violets whom no winds assault because they are content with lowly places; there the myrrh of perfect penance perfumes the air and the incense of constant prayer rises unceasingly. . . .

The Redeemer of the world, at the very beginning of the work of redemption, made His herald a dweller in the desert, so that in the dawn of the new world the morning star of truth might rise from you, after whom was to come the full sun who was to bring light to the world's darkness by the glory of His splendour. You are Jacob's ladder, conveying men to heaven, and bringing angels to our aid. You are the golden highway leading men back to their native land, the racecourse which carries those who have run well onward to receive their crown. O eremitic life, you are the soul's bath, the death of evildoing, the cleanser of filth; you make clean the hidden places of the soul, wash away the foulness of sin and make souls shine with angelic purity. The hermit's cell is the meeting place of God and man, a cross-roads for those who dwell in the flesh and heavenly things. For there the citizens of heaven hold intercourse with men, not in the language of the flesh, but by being made manifest, without any clamour of tongues, to the rich and secret places of the soul. The cell knows those hidden counsels which God gives to men. How fair a thing it is to see a brother in his cell pass all the night in singing psalms, keeping watch, as it were, over God's fortress; as he watches the stars move through their heavenly courses the psalms proceed in order from his lips. And as the earlier and later stars come to light alternating in their courses, so the psalms which proceed from his lips as from a day-spring come to an end as if keeping pace with the movement of the stars. He is carrying out the duty of his calling, and they are performing the task appointed to them; he in his chanting is reaching out inwardly towards the unapproachable light while they, one after the other, refresh his bodily eyes with visible light. And although each hastens towards his end by a different path, yet the heavenly bodies are in harmony with God's servant in their mutual obedience.

ST. PETER DAMIAN [143]

FEBRUARY 22
THE CHAIR OF ST. PETER

Since early times, the Roman Church has had, in addition to the great summer feast of Sts. Peter and Paul (June 29), a special commemoration of the primatial authority of St. Peter. As witness one of the most renowned of the Apostolic Fathers, the Roman See has always held a peculiar place in the affection and obedience of orthodox believers because of its "presiding in love" and service over all the Churches of God.

Epistle to the Romans.

Ignatius, also called Theophoros, to the church that has found mercy in the transcendent Majesty of the Most High Father and of Jesus Christ, His only Son; the church by the will of Him who willed all things that exist, beloved and illuminated through the faith and love of Jesus Christ our God; which also presides in the chief place of the Roman territory; a church worthy of God, worthy of honor, worthy of felicitation, worthy of praise, worthy of success, worthy of sanctification, and presiding in love, maintaining the law of Christ, and bearer of the Father's name.

ST. IGNATIUS OF ANTIOCH [144]

The Chair of Unity.

Listen: this is the mystery of Catholic unity, and the immortal principle of the Church's beauty. True beauty comes from health; what makes the Church strong, makes her fair: her unity makes her fair, her unity makes her strong. United from within by the Holy Spirit, she has besides a common bond of her outward communion, and must remain united by a government in which the authority of Jesus Christ is represented. Thus one unity guards the other, and, under the seal of ecclesiastical government, the unity of the spirit is preserved. What is this government? What is its form? Let us say nothing of ourselves; let us open the Gospel; the Lamb has opened the seals of that sacred book, and the tradition of the Church has explained all.

We shall find in the Gospel that Jesus Christ, willing to *begin* the mystery of unity in His Church, among all His disciples chose twelve; but that, willing to *consummate* the mystery of unity in the same Church, among the twelve He chose one. *He called His disciples,* said the Gospel; here are all; *and among them He chose twelve.* Here is the first separation, and the Apostles chosen. *And these are the names of the twelve Apostles: the first, Simon, who is called Peter.* [Mt. 10, 1–2] Here, in a second separation, St. Peter is set at the head, and called for that reason by the name of Peter, "which Jesus Christ," says St. Mark, "had given him," in order to prepare, as you will see, the work which He was proposing to raise all His building on that stone.

All this is yet but a beginning of the mystery of unity. Jesus Christ, in beginning it, still spoke to many: *Go, preach; I send you* [see Mt. 28, 19]. Now, when He would put the last hand to the mystery of unity, He speaks no longer to many: He marks out Peter personally, and by the new name which He has given him. It is One who speaks to one: Jesus Christ the Son of God to Simon son of Jonas; Jesus Christ, who is the true Stone, strong of Himself, to Simon, who is only the stone by the strength which Jesus Christ imparts to him. It is to him that Christ speaks, and in speaking acts on him, and stamps upon him His own immovableness. *And I,* He says, *say to you, you are Peter; and,* He adds, *upon this rock I will build my Church, and,* He concludes, *the gates of hell shall not prevail against it.* [Mt. 16, 18] To prepare him for that honour Jesus Christ, who knows that faith in Himself is the foundation of His Church, inspires Peter with a faith worthy to be the foundation of that admirable building. *You are the Christ, the Son of the living God.* [Mt. 16, 16] By that bold preaching of the faith he draws to himself the inviolable promise which makes him the foundation of the Church. The word of Jesus Christ, who out of nothing makes what pleases Him, gives this strength to a mortal. Say not, think not, that this ministry of St. Peter terminates with him: that which is to serve for support to an eternal Church can never have an end. Peter will live in his successors. Peter will always speak in his chair. This is what the Fathers say. This is what six hundred and thirty Bishops at the Council of Chalcedon confirm.

But consider briefly what follows—Jesus Christ pursues His design; and, after having said to Peter, the eternal preacher of the faith, *You are Peter, and upon this rock I will build my Church,* He adds: *And I will give to you the keys of the kingdom of heaven.* [Mt. 16, 19] You, who have the prerogative of preaching the faith, you shall have likewise the keys which mark the authority of government: *What you shall bind on earth shall be bound in heaven: and what you shall loose on earth shall be loosed in heaven.* [Mt. 16, 19] *All is subjected to these keys: all, my brethren, kings and nations, pastors and flocks: we declare it with joy, for we love unity, and hold obedience to be our glory. It is Peter who is ordered first to love more than all the other Apostles, and then "to feed," and govern all, both "the lambs and the sheep," the young ones, and the mothers, and the pastors themselves: pastors in regard to the people, and sheep in regard to Peter. In him they honour Jesus Christ, confessing likewise that with reason greater love is asked of him, forasmuch as he has a greater dignity with a greater charge; and that among us, under the discipline of a Master such as ours, according to His word it must be, that the first be as He, by charity the servant of all.*

Thus St. Peter appears the first in all things: the first to confess the faith; the first in the obligation to exercise love; the first of all the Apostles who saw Jesus Christ risen, as he was to be the first witness of it before all the people; the first when the number of the Apostles was to be filled up; the first who confirmed the faith by a miracle; the first to convert the Jews; the first to receive the Gentiles; the first everywhere.

You have seen this unity in the Holy See, would you see it in the whole episcopal order and college? Still it is in St. Peter that it must appear, and still in these words: *Whatsoever you shall bind shall be bound; whatsoever you shall loose shall be loosed.* All the Popes and all the holy Fathers have taught it with a common consent. Yes, my brethren, these great words, in which you have seen so clearly the Primacy of St. Peter, have set up Bishops, since the force of their ministry consists in binding or loosing those who believe or believe not their word. Thus this divine power of binding and loosing is a necessary annexment, and, as it were, the final seal of the preaching which Jesus Christ has entrusted to them; and you see, in passing, the whole order of ecclesiastical jurisdiction. Therefore, the same who said to Peter: *Whatsoever you shall bind shall be bound; whatsoever you shall loose shall be loosed,* has said the same thing to all the Apostles, and has said to them, moreover: *Whosesoever sins you remit, they shall be remitted; and whosesoever sins you retain, they shall be retained.* [Jn. 20, 23] What is to bind, but to retain? What to loose, but to remit? And the same who gives to Peter this power, gives it also with His own mouth to all the Apostles: *As my Father has sent me, so, says He, I send you.* [Jn. 20, 21] A power better established, or a mission more immediate, cannot be seen. So He breathes equally on all. On all He diffuses the same

Spirit with that breath, in saying: *Receive you the Holy Ghost,* and the rest that we have quoted.

It was, then, clearly the design of Jesus Christ to put first in one alone, what afterwards He meant to put in several; but the sequence does not reverse the beginning, nor the first lose his place. That first word, *Whatsoever you shall bind,* said to one alone, has already ranged under his power each one of those to whom shall be said, *Whatsoever you shall remit;* for the promises of Jesus Christ, as well as His gift, are without repentance; and what is once given indefinitely and universally is irrevocable. Besides, that power given to several carries its restriction in its division, while power given to one alone, and over all, and without exception, carries with it plenitude, and, not having to be divided with any other, it has no bounds save those which its terms convey.

JACQUES BOSSUET [145]

FEBRUARY 24
ST. MATTHIAS

The apostolate is not a human undertaking in which devotion, tact, and intelligence suffice. Help me, God, to understand that above all the apostolate asks that I completely abandon myself to your will, that I let you act in and through me.

MARCEL LEGAUT [146]

What is an apostle really? Frankly, the impression we get from the New Testament hardly permits us to claim that these men were great or ingenious in the wordly sense. It is difficult even to count them "great religious personalities," if by this we mean bearers of inherent spiritual talents. John and Paul were probably exceptions, but we only risk misunderstanding them both by overstating this. On the whole, we do the apostle no service by considering him a great religious personality. This attitude is usually the beginning of unbelief. Personal importance, spiritual creativeness, dynamic faith are not decisive in his life. What counts is that Jesus Christ has called him, pressed his seal upon him, and sent him forth.

You have not chosen me, but I have chosen you, and have appointed you that you should go and bear fruit . . . [Jn. 15, 16] An apostle then is one who is sent. It is not he who speaks, but Christ in him. In his first Corinthian epistle Paul distinguishes nicely between the instructions of "the Lord" and what he, Paul, has to say. The Lord's words are commands; his own, suggestions. The apostle is filled with Christ, saturated with thought of Christ; the Lord, whom he represents, is the substance of his life. What he teaches is not what he has learned from personal "experience" or "revelation," it is God's word, uttered upon God's command: *Go, therefore, and make disciples of all nations . . . teaching them to observe all that I have commanded you.* [Mt. 28, 19] To this end alone has the apostle been called, and his very limitations seem an added protection to the truth he bears. When Jesus says: *I praise you, Father, Lord of heaven and earth, that you did hide these things from the wise and prudent, and did reveal them to little ones* [Mt. 11, 25], it is an outburst of jubilation over the unutterable mystery of God's love and creative glory. Spiritually, the apostle is seldom more than a "little one"; precisely this guarantees the purity of his role of messenger.

To be nothing in oneself, everything in Christ; to be obliged to contain such tremendous contents in so small a vessel; to be a constant herald with no life of one's own; to forego once and forever the happy unity of blood and heart and spirit in all one does and is—something of the trials of such an existence dawns on us when we read the first letter of St. Paul to the Corinthians, of that Paul who experienced so deeply the simultaneous greatness and questionableness of apostledom: *For I think God has set forth us the apostles last of all, as men doomed to death, seeing that we have been made a spectacle to the world, and to angels, and to men. We are fools for Christ, but you are wise in Christ! We are weak, but you are strong! You are honored, but we are without honor! To this very hour we hunger and thirst, and we are naked and buffeted, and have no fixed abode. And we toil, working with our own hands. We are reviled and we bless, we are persecuted and we bear it, we are maligned and we entreat, we have become as the refuse of this world, as the offscouring of all, even until now!* [1 Cor. 4, 8–13]

ROMANO GUARDINI [147]

Let someone else take his place. (Epistle)

What solemn overpowering thoughts must have crowded on St. Matthias, when he received the greetings of the eleven Apostles, and took his seat among them as their brother! His very election was a witness against himself if he did not fulfil it. And such surely will ours be in our degree. We take the place of others who have gone before, as Matthias did; we are "baptized for the dead," filling up the ranks of soldiers, some of whom, indeed, have fought a good fight, but many of whom in every age have made void their calling. Many are called, few are chosen. The monuments of sin and unbelief are set up around us. The casting away of the Jews was the reconciling of the Gentiles. The fall of one nation is the conversion of another. The Church loses old branches, and gains new. God works according to His own inscrutable pleasure; He has left the East, and manifested Himself Westward. Thus the Christian of every age is but the successor of the lost and of the dead. How long we of this country shall be put in trust with the Gospel, we know not; but while we have the privilege, assuredly we do but stand in the place of Christians who have either utterly fallen away, or are so corrupted as scarcely to let their light shine before men. We are at present witnesses of the Truth; and our very glory is our warning. By the superstitions, the profanities, the indifference, the unbelief of the world called Christian, we are called upon to be lowly-minded while we preach aloud, and to tremble while we rejoice. Let us then, as a Church and as individuals, one and all, look to Him who alone can keep us from falling. Let us with single heart look up to Christ our Saviour, and put ourselves into His hands, from whom all our strength and wisdom is derived.

JOHN HENRY NEWMAN [148]

March

Sts. Perpetua and Felicity
St. Thomas Aquinas

MARCH 6

STS. PERPETUA AND FELICITY

The persecution of Emperor Septimius Severus was an attempt to prevent further conversions to Christianity. At Carthage in the beginning of 203 A.D., *five catechumens, among them two young women, one of noble birth, Perpetua, one her slave girl, Felicity, were apprehended and imprisoned. The following account is partly from Perpetua's diary, partly from that of an eyewitness recital of the actual martyrdom.*

All the members of Perpetua's family seemed to have sympathized with her except her father.

While we were still under watch my father attempted to persuade me, for the sake of his affection for me, to renounce my proposed confession. And I said to him, "Father, do you see that household utensil lying there?" and he replied, "I do." "Can you call that thing there anything but a pitcher?" "No," he said. "Neither can I call myself anything else than what I am, a Christian." Then my father, provoked at my words, rushed at me as if he would tear my eyes out. But he only cried aloud and went away vanquished, carried away with his devil's arguments. Then, while he was from home for a few days, I gave thanks to the Lord and his absence became a source of consolation to me. In the meantime we were baptized; and I was prompted by the Holy Spirit to ask nothing from the water of baptism except patient endurance of the flesh.

After a few days we were cast into prison, and I was very much afraid. How dreadful a day! for never had I seen such darkness and excessive heat. For the prison was crowded with a multitude of people, chiefly on account of false accusations of the soldiers. Besides all these things, I was distressed on account of my infant child. Then Tertius and Pomponius, blessed deacons who ministered to us, arranged by paying gratuities that we should be transferred to a milder quarter of the prison. Then all went out and attended to their wants; I suckled my child, which was now enfeebled with hunger; I talked with my mother, I cheered my brother, I commended to them my child. But I was consumed with grief because I saw them grieving on my account. Such solicitude I suffered many days. But I obtained leave for my child to remain in the prison with me; and then I grew strong and was freed from distress and anxiety about my child, and lo! the prison became to me a palace, so that I preferred to be there to being elsewhere.

ST. PERPETUA [149]

Her father again besieges her.

After a few days we learned that we were to have a hearing. My father also arrived from his long journey, worn out, and coming to me urged me to abandon my confession, saying, "Have pity, my daughter, on my gray hairs, have pity on your father, if indeed I am worthy to be called father by you. Remember that with these hands I have brought you up to this flower of your age and preferred you to all your brothers. Do not bring shame on me in the sight of men. Have regard to your brothers, have regard to your mother and your mother's sister, have regard to your son, who will not be able to live after you. Lay aside your courage and do not bring us all to destruction, for none of us will ever speak freely again if any harm should come to you."

So said my father in his affection, kissing my hands and throwing himself at my feet, and with tears he called me, not Daughter, but Lady. And I grieved at my father's state, that he alone of my whole family did not rejoice at my suffering. And I comforted him, saying, "At the judge's tribunal whatever God wills will happen, for be sure that we shall be not in our own power but in that of God." And he departed from me in sorrow.

Another day, while we were at dinner, we were suddenly hurried away to our hearing; and when we had come into the market-place, at once a report went about the neighboring parts and there ran together a very great crowd. And when we came to the tribunal, the others were examined, and confessed. And as I was about to be examined, my father appeared with my boy and drew me aside and said in a supplicating tone, "Sacrifice, out of pity for the babe!" Then Hilarianus, the procurator, who had just received the power of life and death in place of the proconsul Minucius Timinianus, who had died, said, "Spare the gray hairs of your father, spare the infancy of your child; offer sacrifice for the welfare of the emperors." And I replied, "I will not sacrifice." Hilarianus said, "Are you a Christian?" and I answered, "I am a Christian."

When my father kept trying to seduce me from the faith, Hilarianus ordered him to be put out, and some of the guards beat him with their rods. And it grieved me as if I had been beaten myself, for I pitied his wretched old age. Then the procurator condemned us all to the beasts, and with joy we went down to the prison. Now since the child was fed at my breast and was accustomed to stay with me in prison, I sent Pomponius the deacon to my father to ask for the babe. But he refused to give it up. Yet, as God ordered, the child from that time did not desire the breast, nor did my breast cause me trouble, in order perhaps that I might not be troubled both by anxiety for the child and pain in the breasts.

ST. PERPETUA [150]

After a few days Pudens, a soldier, who had charge of the prison, began to regard us with much esteem, perceiving that the great power of God was in us, and he admitted many brethren to see us, so that they and we were mutually refreshed. And when the day of the exhibition drew near, my father came to me worn with grief and began to pluck out his beard and throw himself on the ground, and lying on his face, to reproach his years with such words and accusations as might move all creation. And I grieved for his unhappy old age.

These things I have written up to the day before the exhibition.

What shall take place in the amphitheatre, let him describe who will.

ST. PERPETUA [151]

The day of martyrdom, March 7, 203.

Finally the day of their triumph dawned and they went forth from their prison to the amphitheatre as if to heaven, glad and radiant of countenance, their hearts beating with joy rather than with fear. Perpetua brought up the rear, walking composedly . . . and by her piercing gaze forcing the spectators to drop their eyes. Felicity, too, rejoiced to come from the delivery of her child to the arena, to be washed after childbearing with a second baptism.

After the men are delivered to the beasts it is the turn of the women.

For the women a savage cow had been reserved. . . . Perpetua was tossed first and fell on her side. But as soon as she could sit up she noticed that her tunic was torn down one side and quickly pulled it together about her thinking more of her modesty than of her pain. Then she tidied up her dishevelled hair lest she appear to be mourning in the midst of her glorious passion. Finally she arose and seeing that Felicity had been tossed by the cow went to help her up. Seeing them both on their feet the savage crowd decided it had had enough and they were led toward the exit gate. . . .

[But this was merely a reprieve for] the people began to clamor for their return to the center of the arena so that they could see them receive the death stroke. . . .

Of their own accord the martyrs walked to where the crowd wanted them, but first they exchanged the kiss of peace that they might conclude their martyrdom with the customary liturgical rites. Standing there quietly they awaited the thrust of the gladiator's sword. . . . Perpetua received the first stroke between the ribs. In her pain she screamed and then siezing the shaking hand of the unpracticed gladiator herself guided the sword to her own throat. Perhaps such a woman, so feared by the devil, could not have been killed unless she had willed it.

PASSION OF ST. PERPETUA [152]

MARCH 7

ST. THOMAS AQUINAS

Everyone knows the influence Thomas's genius has had on the intellectual life of the Church. An extremely controversial figure in the thirteenth century, his remarkable theological syntheses gradually imposed themselves in large measure on the great theological schools of Christendom. In modern times his thought has experienced a new revival, and for many Catholic thinkers he is still the prince of theologians. Modern popes since Leo XIII have considered him the common doctor of the schools and have worked to make his philosophical and theological system the basis of seminary instruction.

The Common Doctor.

Now above all the Doctors of the Schools towers the figure of Thomas Aquinas, the leader and master of them all, who, as Cajetan observes, "because he had the utmost reverence for the Doctors of antiquity, seems to have inherited in a way the intellect of all." Thomas gathered their doctrines together—they had long lain dispersed like the scattered limbs of a body—and knitted them into one whole. He disposed them in marvellous order and increased them to such an extent that he is rightly and deservedly considered the pre-eminent guardian and glory of the Catholic Church.

JACQUES MARITAIN [153]

The possibilities of the human mind.

It is the nature of the human mind to gather its knowledge from sensible things; nor can it of itself arrive at the direct vision of the divine substance, as that substance is in itself raised above all sensible things and all other beings to boot, and beyond all proportion with them. But because the perfect good of man consists in his knowing God in such way as he can, there is given man a way of ascending to the knowledge of God, to the end that so noble a creature should not seem to exist altogether in vain, unable to attain the proper end of his existence. The way is this, that as all the perfections of creatures descend in order from God, who is the height of perfection, man should begin from the lower creatures, and ascend by degrees, and so advance to the knowledge of God. Of this descent of perfections from God there are two processes. One is on the part of the first origin of things: for the divine wisdom, to make things perfect, produced them in order, that the universe might consist of a complete round of creatures from highest to lowest. The other process belongs to the things themselves: for, as causes are nobler than effects, the first and highest products of causation, while falling short of the First Cause, which is God, nevertheless are superior to the effects which they themselves produce; and so on in order, until we come to the lowest of creatures. And because in that "roof and crown of all things" (*summo rerum vertice*), God, we find the most perfect unity; and everything is stronger and more excellent, the more thoroughly it is one; it follows that diversity and variety increase in things, the further they are removed from Him who is the first principle of all. Therefore the process of derivation of creatures from their first principle may be represented by a sort of pyramid, with unity at the apex, and the widest multiplicity at the base. And thus in the diversity of things there is apparent a diversity of ways, beginning from one principle and terminating in different terms. By these ways then our understanding can ascend to God.

But the weakness of our understanding prevents us from knowing these ways perfectly. Our knowledge begins with sense; and sense is concerned with exterior accidents (phenomena), which are of themselves sensible, as colour, smell, and the like. With difficulty can our mind penetrate through such exterior phenomena to an inner knowledge of things, even where it perfectly grasps by sense their accidents. Much less will it be able to attain to a comprehension of the natures of those objects of which we perceive only a few phenomena by sense; and still less of those natures no accidents of which lie open to sense, but certain effects which they produce, inadequate to their power, enable us to recognise them. But even though the very natures of things were known to us, still we should have but slight knowledge of their order, of their mutual relations, and direction by divine providence to their final end, since we cannot penetrate the plan of Providence. The ways themselves then being so imperfectly known to us, how shall we travel by them to any perfect knowledge of the First Beginning of all things, which transcends all created ways and is out of all proportion with them? Even though we knew the said ways perfectly, we should still fall short of perfect knowledge of their origin and starting point.

Feeble and inadequate then being any knowledge to which man could arrive by these ways, God has revealed to men facts about Himself which surpass human understanding; in which revelation there is observed an order of gradual transition from imperfect to perfect. In man's present state, in which his understanding is tied to sense, his mind cannot possibly be elevated to any clear discernment of truths that surpass all proportions of sense: in that state the revelation is given him, not to be understood, but to be heard and believed. Only when he is delivered from the thraldom of sensible things, will he be elevated to an intuition of revealed truth. Thus there is a threefold knowledge that man may have of divine things. The first is an ascent through creatures to the knowledge of God by the natural light of reason. The second is a descent of divine truth by revelation to us; truth exceeding human understanding; truth accepted, not as demonstrated to sight, but as orally delivered for belief. The third is an elevation of the human mind to a perfect insight into things revealed.

ST. THOMAS AQUINAS [154]

The bow in the clouds.

Ecce ponam arcum meum in nubibus—"Behold, I set my bow in the clouds." [Gn. 9, 13] Man's entire path lies among clouds. Never a day when his intellectual sky is clear and the sun visible.

Only an evershifting cloudland—now dark with lowering storm clouds, now the breaking tempest, now a leaden expanse of dull monotony, now mist and driving rain, or again higher and whiter clouds, bright with the light of the sun they veil. But they never disperse, and if there is a passing rift it is night, and we see only stars. For our very essence is set between being and nonentity—the Absolute Being of God and its polar antithesis, the nothingness from which He drew us.

E. I. WATKIN [155]

A humanism of the Incarnation.

Against the old scholasticism, incapable of recognizing in him the true heir of Augustine, he defends the rights of truth in the natural sphere and the value of reason; against the Averroists, incapable of recognizing in him the true interpreter of Aristotle, he defends the rights of revealed truth and the value of faith. Affirming both the essential naturality of metaphysics and the essential *super*naturality of the infused virtues, and the essential subordination of the natural to the supernatural, proclaiming both that grace perfects, without destroying, nature and that the specifically divine life, which grace implants in us, can alone heal the wounds of nature and must take hold of nature absolutely, his peculiar achievement was to bring all the virtues of the mind into the service of Jesus Christ. The whole problem of culture and humanism presented itself in him and his answer was: *sanctity*. Man becomes perfect only supernaturally; he develops only on the cross. A humanism is possible, but on condition that its ultimate end is union with God through the humanity of the Mediator and that it proportions its means to that essentially supernatural end, a humanism of the Incarnation: on condition that it orders itself entirely to love and contemplation; that it entirely subordinates, like the holy soul of Thomas Aquinas itself, mere knowledge to wisdom, and metaphysical wisdom to theological widom and theological wisdom to the wisdom of the saints; that it realizes that the form of reason can subject the world only if it is itself subject to the supra-rational and supra-human order of the Holy Ghost and His gifts. Otherwise humanism, even Christian humanism, will inevitably tend to the destruction of man and a universal ruin.

JACQUES MARITAIN [156]

After the death of the Doctor, Brother Reginald, having returned to Naples and resumed his lectures, exclaimed with many tears: "My brothers, while he was still in life, my Master forbade me to disclose the admirable things concerning him whereof I had been witness. One of these things was that he had acquired his science not by human industry, but by the merit of prayer, for whenever he wished to study, discuss, read, write or dictate, he first had recourse to prayer in private, and poured forth his soul with tears in order to discover the divine secrets, and by the merits of this prayer his doubts were removed and he issued therefrom fully instructed."

PETER CALO [157]

Prayer of St. Thomas Aquinas.

Creator, beyond any words of ours to describe!

In the fullness of Your wisdom You have established the three celestial hierarchies of angels and set them in wonderfully ordered array over Your resplendent heaven. Most gloriously You have disposed all parts of the whole universe, You are the true source of light and wisdom, You are their first and final cause.

Pour out now, I beg You, a ray of Your clear light upon my murky understanding, and take from me my doubly dark inheritance of sin and ignorance. You who inspire the speech of little children, guide and teach my tongue now, and let the grace of Your blessing flow upon my lips. Grant me a sharp discernment, a strong memory, a methodical approach to study, a willing and able docility; let me be precise in interpretation and felicitous in choice of words.

Instruct my beginning, direct my progress, and bring my work to its proper finish: You, who are true God and true Man, living and reigning forever!

ST. THOMAS AQUINAS [158]

Abbreviations

ACW	*Ancient Christian Writers*, edited by J. Quasten, Walter Burghardt, and T. C. Lawler, Westminster, The Newman Press, 1946—.
ANCL	*Ante-Nicene Christian Library*, edited by A. Roberts and J. Donaldson, Edinburgh, twenty-four volumes, 1867–1884.
ANF	*The Ante-Nicene Fathers*, Edinburgh edition revised by A. C. Coxe, Buffalo, ten volumes, 1884–1886.
FC	*The Fathers of the Church*, founded by L. Schopp, series editor R. J. Deferrari, Washington, D.C., The Catholic University of America Press, 1948–.

Reference Table

NUMBER		PAGE
1.	Emily Dickinson, *The Complete Poems of Emily Dickinson,* edited by T. H. Johnson, Boston, Little, Brown, 1960, p. 200.	20
2.	Alfred Delp, *The Prison Meditations of Father Delp,* New York, Herder and Herder, 1963, p. 21.	22
3.	St. Cyril of Jerusalem, *The Catechetical Lectures,* number xv, 1, Philadelphia, The Westminster Press, pp. 147–148.	23
4.	Gabriel Marcel, *Homo Viator,* Chicago, Henry Regnery Co., 1951, pp. 49–50.	24
5.	Jean Danielou, *The Advent of Salvation,* New York, Paulist Press, 1962, pp. 118–119.	24
6.	Henri De Lubac, *De la connaissance de Dieu,* Paris, Témoignage Chrétien, 1941, p. 84.	25
7.	Blaise Pascal, *Pensées,* number 194, New York, Random House, 1941, p. 71.	25
8.	Charles Peguy, *Le Porche du Mystère de la deuxième Vertu,* Paris, Gallimard, 1935, pp. 20–22.	26
9.	A. M. Carre, *Hope or Despair,* New York, P. J. Kenedy & Sons, 1955, p. 9.	27
10.	Alban Goodier, *The Public Life of Our Lord Jesus Christ,* volume I, New York, P. J. Kenedy & Sons, 1944, pp. 12–13.	28
11.	Giovanni Papini, *Life of Christ,* New York, Harcourt, Brace, 1923, p. 137.	28

NUMBER		PAGE
12.	Gertrude Von Le Fort, *Hymns to the Church,* New York, Sheed & Ward, 1953, p. 21.	29
13.	Gerald Vann, *The Heart of Man,* New York, Doubleday, 1960, p. 156.	29
14.	Jean Danielou, *The Advent of Salvation,* New York, Paulist Press, 1962, pp. 81–82.	30
15.	St. Irenaeus of Lyons, *Proof of the Apostolic Preaching, ACW* XVI, Westminster, The Newman Press, 1952, p. 69.	31
16.	The Akathistos Hymn, Oxford, Blackfriars, 1947, Oikos I.	32
17.	Max Thurian, *Mary, Mother of All Christians,* New York, Herder and Herder, 1964, pp. 66–67.	33
18.	St. Irenaeus of Lyons, "Against the Heresies," Chapter 3, 22, 4, in J. Quasten, *Patrology,* volume I, Westminster, The Newman Press, 1951, pp. 297–298.	34
19.	Jean Danielou, *The Advent of Salvation,* New York, Paulist Press, 1962, pp. 85–86.	35
20.	Karl Rahner, *The Eternal Year,* Baltimore, Helicon, 1964, pp. 17–18.	37
21.	St. Leo the Great, "Sermon 28 on the Nativity of the Lord (*Cum Semper*) 8," in *Select Sermons of St. Leo the Great on the Incarnation,* London, J. Masters, 1886, pp. 20–21.	38
22.	Romano Guardini, *The Lord,* Chicago, Henry Regnery Co., 1954, p. 24.	39
23.	Roman Martyrology in M. B. Hellriegel, *Vine and Branches,* St. Louis, Pio Decimo Press, 1948, pp. 35–36.	44
24.	Coptic Liturgy, sixth or seventh century (?) in *Early Christian Prayers,* edited by A. Hamman, Chicago, Henry Regnery Co., 1961, p. 76.	44
25.	St. John of the Cross, *The Ascent of Mount Carmel* in H. De Lubac, *The Discovery of God,* New York, P. J. Kenedy & Sons, 1960, p. 191.	45
26.	St. Leo the Great, "Sermon 26 on the Lord's Nativity (*Omnibus*) 6," in *Select Sermons of St.*	

NUMBER PAGE

Leo the Great on the Incarnation, London, J. Masters, 1886, pp. 12–14. 46

27. Romano GUARDINI, *The Lord,* Chicago, Henry Regnery, 1954, pp. 14–15. 47
28. John MILTON, *The Complete Poems of John Milton,* edited by F. A. Patterson, New York, Appleton-Century-Crofts, Inc., 1952, p. 200. 47
29. John Henry Cardinal NEWMAN, *Parochial and Plain Sermons,* volume II, London, Longmans, Green, 1898, pp. 38–40. 49
30. Gerald VANN, *The Eagle's Word,* New York, Harcourt, Brace & World, 1961, p. 106. 49
31. ST. IRENAEUS OF LYONS, *Proof of the Apostolic Preaching, ACW* XVI, Westminster, The Newman Press, 1952, p. 51. 50
32. ST. LEO THE GREAT, "Sermon 63 on the Lord's Passion (*Gloria*) 12," in *Select Sermons of St. Leo the Great on the Incarnation,* London, J. Masters, 1886, pp. 46–47. 50
33. Hugo RAHNER and Karl RAHNER, *Prayers for Meditation,* New York, Herder and Herder, 1963, pp. 20–22. 52
34. Richard VERSTEGAN, "Our Lady's Lullaby," *The Golden Book of Catholic Poetry,* edited by A. Noyes, Philadelphia, J. B. Lippincott, 1946, pp. 65–66. 53
35. ST. PETER CHRYSOLOGUS, "Sermon 154," in *Selected Sermons, FC* XVII, Washington, Catholic University of America Press, 1953, pp. 260–261. 53
36. T. S. ELIOT, *The Complete Poems and Plays,* New York, Harcourt, Brace & World, 1961, pp. 51–52. 54
37. Gerald VANN, *The Eagle's Word,* New York, Harcourt, Brace & World, 1961, pp. 51–52. 55
38. ST. JEROME, "Commentary on the Epistle to the Galatians," Chapter I, 6, *The Roman Breviary,* December 27, Lesson 6. 55
39. John Henry Cardinal NEWMAN, *Parochial and Plain Sermons,* volume II, London, Longmans, Green, 1898, pp. 55–56. 56

NUMBER | PAGE

40. St. John Chrysostom, *Commentary on St. John the Apostle and Evangelist, Homilies,* numbers 1–47, *FC* XLI, Washington, Catholic University of America Press, 1957, pp. 4–6. — 58
41. Alfred Delp, *The Prison Meditations of Father Delp,* New York, Herder and Herder, 1963, pp. 80–81. — 59
42. Robert Southwell, *The Complete Works of Robert Southwell,* London, Burns & Oates, 1894, p. 116. — 59
43. Charles Peguy, *The Mystery of the Holy Innocents,* New York, Harper & Row, 1956, pp. 237–239. — 60
44. St. Thomas of Canterbury, in E. Grim, *Materials for the History of Archbishop Becket,* Rolls Series II, London, 1889, p. 430. — 61
45. John Donne, *Divine Poems,* edited by Helen Gardner, New York, Oxford University Press, 1952, p. 200. — 61
46. Gerard S. Sloyan, *To Hear the Word of God, Homilies at Mass,* New York, Herder and Herder, 1965, pp. 39–40. — 63
47. St. Justin Martyr, "Dialogue with Trypho," Chapter 100 in *The Writings of St. Justin Martyr,* edited by T. Falls, New York, Christian Heritage, 1948, pp. 304–305. — 63
48. St. Leo the Great, "Sermon 64 on the Lord's Passion (*Omnia*)," *Select Sermons of St. Leo the Great on the Incarnation,* London, J. Masters, 1886, pp. 56–58. — 64
49. René Voillaume, "The Time of the Nativity," *Jesus Caritas,* number 18, January, 1964, pp. 28–29. — 66
50. St. Bernard of Clairvaux, "Sermon 15 on the Canticle of Canticles," in *The Roman Breviary,* Feast of the Holy Name of Jesus, Lesson 6. — 66
51. Gerard Manley Hopkins, *Poems,* edited by R. Bridges, New York, Oxford University Press, 1948, p. 185. — 67
52. Alfred Delp, *The Prison Meditations of Father Delp,* New York, Herder and Herder, 1963, p. 98. — 68

NUMBER | PAGE

53. St. Augustine, "Sermon 200 for the Epiphany," in *Sermons on the Liturgical Seasons, FC* XXXVIII, Washington, Catholic University of America Press, 1959, pp. 63–64, 66. — 69
54. St. Leo the Great, "Sermon 36 on the Feast of the Epiphany (*Dies*) 6," in *Select Sermons of St. Leo the Great on the Incarnation,* London, J. Masters, 1886, pp. 31–32. — 70
55. Robert Southwell, *The Complete Works of Robert Southwell,* London, Burns & Oates, 1894, pp. 113–114. — 71
56. Stanislas Lyonnet, "The Saving Justice of God," in *Theology Digest* 7, 2, Spring, 1960, p. 80. — 72
57. St. John Chrysostom, *Baptismal Instructions, ACW* XXXI, Westminster, The Newman Press, 1963, pp. 315–316. — 72
58. Jesus Caritas Directory, *The Charles of Jesus Secular Fraternity,* Washington, Jesus Caritas, n.d., p. 40. — 73
59. Pope John XXIII, "Pope John on Pastoral Liturgy," in *Worship* 38, August-September, 1963, p. 480. — 74
60. Blaise Pascal, *Pensées,* number 527, New York, Random House, 1941, p. 169. — 74
61. St. Cyril of Jerusalem, *The Catechetical Lectures* III, 11, 14, *LCC* IV, Philadelphia, The Westminster Press, 1955, pp. 95–96, 96–97. — 75
62. Vespers of Epiphany, *Divine Prayers and Service of the Catholic Orthodox Church of Christ,* New York, 1961, pp. 456–57. — 76
63. Charles Burgard, *Scripture in the Liturgy,* Westminster, The Newman Press, 1960, p. 26. — 76
64. Ambrosian Liturgy in *Early Christian Prayers,* edited by A. Hamman, Chicago, Henry Regnery Co., 1961, p. 248. — 77
65. St. Jerome, *The Satirical Letters of St. Jerome,* Chicago, Henry Regnery Co., 1956, pp. 60–61. — 80
66. François Mauriac, *The Life of Jesus,* New York, David McKay, 1937, pp. 28–29. — 81

NUMBER PAGE

67. Gerald VANN, *The Eagle's Word,* New York, Harcourt, Brace & World, 1961, pp. 108–109. 81
68. TERTULLIAN, *To His Wife, ACW* XIII, Westminster, The Newman Press, 1951, pp. 35–36. 82
69. John Henry Cardinal NEWMAN, *Parochial and Plain Sermons,* volume II, London, Longmans, Green, 1898, pp. 57–58. 83
70. TERTULLIAN, *De Corona* 11, *ANF* XI, pp. 347–49. 85
71. Hugo RAHNER and Karl RAHNER, *Prayers for Meditation,* New York, Herder and Herder, 1963, pp. 15–16. 86
72. Romano GUARDINI, *The Lord,* Chicago, Henry Regnery Co., 1954, pp. 50–52. 87
73. Bernard HARING, *Christian Renewal in a Changing World,* New York, Desclee, 1964, p. 208. 88
74. Sigrid UNDSET, *Kristin Lavransdatter,* New York, Alfred A. Knopf, 1954, pp. 1044–1045. 89
75. Walter HILTON, *The Ladder of Perfection,* volume I, 49, Baltimore, Penquin Books, 1957, p. 61. 89
76. TERTULLIAN, *De Corona* 3, *ANF* XI, p. 336. 90
77. ST. AUGUSTINE, *Treatises on Various Subjects, FC* XVI, Washington, Catholic University of America Press, 1952, pp. 39–40. 91
78. ST. AUGUSTINE, "Commentary on Psalm 51:4," in *An Augustine Synthesis,* edited E. Przywara, New York, Sheed & Ward, 1939, p. 271. 91
79. Charles PEGUY, *Fernand Laudet, un nouveau théologien,* Paris, Gallimard, tenth edition, p. 203. 92
80. Karl ADAM, *The Spirit of Catholicism,* New York, Doubleday, 1954, pp. 229–30. 92
81. Jacques B. BOSSUET, *Lettres à une demoiselle de Metz,* 4 lettre., edited by Lachat, Paris, Vivès, 1864, p. 308. 93
82. ST. GREGORY NAZIANZEN, "Discourse 31," 25–27, in H. De Lubac, *Catholicism,* New York, New American Library, 1964, pp. 260–262. 94
83. Robert H. BENSON, *The Religion of the Plain Man,*

New York, Benziger Brothers, 1906, pp. 76–77, 87–89. 96

84. John ECKHART, in *The Soul Afire,* edited by H. A. Reinhold, New York, Meridian Books, 1960, p. 62. 101

85. Blessed Henry SUSO, "Sermon 5," in *The Exemplar,* volume II, Dubuque, The Priory Press, 1962, pp. 325–326. 103

86. ST. AUGUSTINE, *The Works of Aurelius Augustine,* volume IX, Edinburgh, T. & T. Clark, 1875–1892, pp. 318–319. 104

87. John Henry Cardinal NEWMAN, *Faith and Prejudice,* edited by The Birmingham Oratory, New York, Sheed & Ward, 1956, pp. 38–40. 105

88. ST. JOHN CHRYSOSTOM, *On the Priesthood,* Westminster, The Newman Press, 1943, pp. 97–99, 101–102. 107

89. Graham GREENE, *The Power and the Glory,* New York, The Viking Press, 1958, pp. 283–284. 108

90. Romano GUARDINI, *The Living God,* New York, Pantheon, 1957, pp. 77–78. 108

91. Giacomo Cardinal LERCARO, Speech of December 22, 1962, in *The Catholic Worker,* September, 1963, p. 8. 109

92. THE ANCRENE RIWLE, London, Burns & Oates, 1955, pp. 170–171. 110

93. Jacques MARITAIN, "That Suffer Persecution. . . ," in *The Commonweal Reader,* edited by E. S. Skillin, New York, Harper & Brothers, 1949, pp. 148–149. 111

94. Michel QUOIST, "Prayers," in *The Gift of Friendship,* Washington, D. C., *Jesus Caritas,* 1958, pp. 102–104. 113

95. Jean ANOUILH, "Dialogue of Monsieur Vincent," in *Jesus Caritas,* October, 1958, p. 96. 113

96. Paul CLAUDEL, "The Black Pearl," in *Jesus Caritas,* October, 1958, p. 99. 113

97. John Henry Cardinal NEWMAN, *Faith and Prejudice,*

NUMBER		PAGE
	edited by The Birmingham Oratory, New York, Sheed & Ward, 1956, pp. 60–61.	114
98.	Søren KIERKEGAARD, *Fear and Trembling,* New York, Doubleday, 1953, p. 35.	115
99.	Pierre TEILHARD DE CHARDIN, *The Divine Milieu,* New York, Harper & Brothers, 1960, p. 79.	115
100.	George MACDONALD, *George MacDonald, An Anthology,* number 2, edited by C. S. Lewis, New York, Macmillan, 1947, p. 23.	118
101.	Edmund CAMPION, "The Brag," in E. Waugh, *Edmund Campion, Jesuit and Martyr,* New York, Doubleday, 1956, pp. 193–196.	130
102.	Henry WALPOLE, "The Martyrdom of Father Campion," in *The Golden Book of Catholic Poetry,* edited by A. Noyes, Philadelphia, J. B. Lippincott, 1946, pp. 90–91.	131
103.	St. Francis XAVIER in H. J. Coleridge, *The Life and Letters of St. Francis Xavier,* London, Burns & Oates, 1876.	135
104.	ST. PETER CHRYSOLOGUS, "Sermon 67," in *Selected Sermons, FC* XVII, Washington, Catholic University of America Press, 1953, pp. 115–118.	138
105.	Jacobus DE VARAGINE, *The Golden Legend,* as Englished by W. Caxton, volume II, London, J. M. Dent, 1900, pp. 110–111, 112–113, 117.	140
106.	VESPERS OF ST. NICHOLAS, *Divine Prayers and Service of the Catholic Orthodox Church of Christ,* New York, 1961, p. 353.	140
107.	ST. AUGUSTINE, *Confessions,* Chapter VI, 33, New York, New American Library, 1963, p. 114.	141
108.	ST. AMBROSE OF MILAN, "Letter LI to Theodosius," in *Letters, FC* XXVI, Washington, Catholic University of America Press, 1954, pp. 21–22, 23–25.	143
109.	ST. AUGUSTINE, *Confessions,* Chapter IX, 6–7, New York, New American Library, 1963, pp. 193–194.	144
110.	ST. AMBROSE OF MILAN, *Hymnus ad Galli Cantum,* stanzas 1–8, *Hymns and Poems,* 1849.	145

NUMBER PAGE

111. Emile MERSCH, *The Theology of the Mystical Body,* St. Louis, B. Herder, 1951, pp. 179–180. 148
112. Karl RAHNER, *Mary, Mother of the Lord,* New York, Herder and Herder, 1963, pp. 48–50. 149
113. Richard CRASHAW, *The Religious Poems of Richard Crashaw,* edited by R. Shepherd, St. Louis, B. Herder, 1914, pp. 88–89. 150
114. ST. GREGORY THE GREAT, "Homily 26 on the Gospel," in *The Roman Breviary,* December 21, Lesson 7. 150
115. ST. AUGUSTINE, *Sermons on the Liturgical Season, FC* XXXVIII, Washington, Catholic University of America Press, 1959, p. 367. 151
116. John Henry NEWMAN, *Sermons Preached on Various Occasions,* London, Longmans, Green, 1900, pp. 70–72. 153
117. ST. ATHANASIUS, *The Life of Saint Antony, ACW* X, Westminster, The Newman Press, 1950, pp. 22–23. 156
118. ST. ATHANASIUS, *ibid.,* p. 57. 157
119. ST. ATHANASIUS, *ibid.,* pp. 95–96. 158
120. Pope ADRIAN VI in Robert E. McNally, *Reform of the Church,* New York, Herder and Herder, 1963, pp. 115–116. 160
121. CONSILIUM DE EMENDANDA ECCLESIA, *ibid.,* pp. 120–121. 161
122. Reginald Cardinal POLE in Henry St. John, *Essays in Christian Unity,* Westminster, The Newman Press, 1955, p. 12. 161
123. POPE PAUL VI, "Opening Address, Vatican II, September 29, 1963," in *The Pittsburgh Catholic,* October 3, 1963, p. 5. 162
124. John A. MACKAY, *Ecumenics, The Science of the Church Universal,* Englewood Cliffs, N.J., Prentice-Hall, pp. 65–66. 163
125. Karl ADAM, *One and Holy,* New York, Sheed & Ward, 1951, p. 130. 163
126. ST. METHODIUS, *The Symposium, ACW* XXVII, Westminster, The Newman Press, 1958, p. 99. 164

NUMBER		PAGE
127.	St. Methodius, *ibid.*, p. 157.	164
128.	Prudentius, volume II, Cambridge, The Harvard University Press, 1958, pp. 339–343.	166
129.	St. Ambrose of Milan, *Letters, FC* XXVI, Washington, Catholic University of America Press, 1954, p. 299.	166
130.	Henri Daniel-Rops, *St. Paul, Apostle of Nations,* Notre Dame, Fides, 1953, pp. 26, 27–28, 30–31.	168
131.	E. Schillebeeckx, O.P., *Christ the Sacrament of the Encounter with God,* New York, Sheed & Ward, 1963, pp. 182–183.	169
132.	The Martyrdom of St. Polycarp, *ACW* VI, Westminster, The Newman Press, 1948, pp. 90, 94–99.	172
133.	Henri Daniel-Rops, *Les saints de tous les jours,* Grenoble-Paris, Arthaud, 1949, p. 213.	173
134.	St. John Chrysostom, *Homily 20,* Library of the Fathers.	176
135.	St. Francis de Sales, *Selected Letters,* New York, Harper & Row, 1960, pp. 57–60.	179
136.	St. Francis de Sales, *ibid.*, p. 144.	180
137.	Henri Gheon, *The Secret of Saint John Bosco,* New York, Sheed & Ward, 1936, pp. 194–197.	182
138.	St. Ignatius of Antioch, *The Epistles of St. Clement of Rome and St. Ignatius of Antioch, ACW* I, Westminster, The Newman Press, 1946, pp. 61–62.	184
139.	St. Ignatius of Antioch, *ibid.*, p. 71.	185
140.	St. Ignatius of Antioch, *ibid.*, pp. 81–83.	186
141.	John O'Donnell, "The Purification," in *Worship* 38, January, 1964, pp. 72, 76.	187
142.	Yves M.-J. Congar, *The Mystery of the Temple,* Westminster, The Newman Press, 1962, pp. 119–120.	189
143.	St. Peter Damian, *Selected Writings on the Spiritual Life,* New York, Harper & Row, 1959, pp. 74, 76–77.	190
144.	St. Ignatius of Antioch, *The Epistle of St. Clement of Rome and St. Ignatius of Antioch, ACW* I, Westminster, The Newman Press, 1946, p. 80.	191

NUMBER		PAGE
145.	Jacques B. BOSSUET in T. W. Allies, *The See of St. Peter,* London, Catholic Truth Society, 1917, pp. 30–35.	194
146.	Marcel LEGAUT, *Prières d'un croyant,* Paris, Grosset, 1947, p. 233.	194
147.	Romano GUARDINI, *The Lord,* Chicago, Henry Regnery Co., 1954, pp. 67–68.	196
148.	John Henry Cardinal NEWMAN, *Parochial and Plain Sermons,* volume II, London, Longmans, Green, 1898, pp. 124–125.	198
149.	ST. PERPETUA in F. Palmer, *Heretics, Saints and Martyrs,* Cambridge, The Harvard University Press, 1925, pp. 189–90.	199
150.	ST. PERPETUA, *ibid.,* pp. 192–193.	200
151.	ST. PERPETUA, *ibid.,* pp. 195–196.	201
152.	"Passion de sainte Perpétue et de ses compagnons," *La vraie légende dorée,* Paris, Payot, 1928, pp. 167–187 *passim.*	202
153.	Jacques MARITAIN, *St. Thomas Aquinas, Angel of the Schools,* London, Sheed & Ward, 1946, p. 146.	202
154.	ST. THOMAS AQUINAS, *Of God and His Creatures,* edited by J. Rickaby, Westminster, Carroll Press (Newman), 1950, pp. 337–339.	204
155.	E. I. WATKIN, *The Bow in the Clouds,* New York, Sheed & Ward, 1931, p. 1.	205
156.	Jacques MARITAIN, *St. Thomas Aquinas, Angel of the Schools,* London, Sheed & Ward, 1946, pp. 19–20.	206
157.	Peter CALO, *Vita sancti Thomae Aquinatis* in J. and R. Maritain, *Prayer and Intelligence,* New York, Sheed & Ward, 1943, p. xi.	206
158.	ST. THOMAS AQUINAS in J. Pieper and H. Raskop, *What Catholics Believe,* New York, Pantheon, 1951, p. 1.	206